the buddha next door

the buddha next door

ordinary people, extraordinary stories

zan gaudioso *and* greg martin

MIDDLEWAY
P R E S S

Santa Monica, CA

Published by Middleway Press

A division of the SGI-USA

606 Wilshire Blvd., Santa Monica, CA 90401

© 2007 SGI-USA

ISBN 978-0-9779245-1-6

Cover and interior design by Lightbourne, Inc.

10 9 8 7 6 5 4 3 2 1

Library of Congress Cataloging-in-Publication Data

The Buddha next door : ordinary people, extraordinary stories / Zan
Gaudioso, Greg Martin.
        p. cm.
    ISBN 978-0-9779245-1-6 (pbk. : alk. paper)
    1. Soka Gakkai Buddhists—Biography. 2. Spiritual biography.
    3. Religious life—Soka Gakkai. I. Gaudioso, Zan. II. Martin, Greg
BQ8448.B83 2007
294.3'9280922—dc22
[B]
                                        2007014895

table of contents

3 career and success   91

4 finances   135

preface

*If there is any religion that could
cope with modern scientific needs
it would be Buddhism.*
—ALBERT EINSTEIN

THE BUDDHA IN YOUR MIRROR—best-selling introduction to Nichiren Buddhist practice tells us, "Never before in the history of the West have so many people turned to the timeless wisdom of Buddhism for answers to the great questions of life as well as to master the problems of daily existence." The obvious sequel to *The Buddha In Your Mirror*—Buddhism explained—is *The Buddha Next Door*, Buddhism lived.

In this book we open windows into the lives of people who have made what *The Buddha In Your Mirror* calls "the thrilling leap from the mere holding of knowledge to the actualization of our vast potential." In *The Buddha Next Door* you will read accounts of how people are changing their lives and circumstances for the better, how they are incorporating the wisdom of ancient teachers

1

into their lives in the twenty-first century.

Let's take a brief detour at this point in the story to provide some background information and terminology that will help you better grasp the stories that will come.

HISTORY

Born twenty-five hundred years ago, Siddhartha, later known as Shakyamuni Buddha, brought Buddhism into being through his own enlightenment. Making Buddhism even more accessible to people, Nichiren Daishonin, born in Japan in 1222, gave concrete and practical expression to the Buddha's philosophy by expressing his central teachings in a prayer, an invocation, based on the title of the Lotus Sutra, the most important and influential scripture of Mahayana Buddhism.

Nichiren defined the essence of this teaching as Nam-myoho-renge-kyo (see pronunciation guide, page 298). *Nam* derives from Sanskrit. A close translation of its meaning is "to devote oneself." *Myoho* literally means the Mystic Law and expresses the relationship between the life inherent in the universe and the many different ways this life expresses itself. *Renge* means lotus flower. The lotus blooms and produces fruit at the same time and thus represents the simultaneity of cause and effect. *Kyo* literally means sutra, the voice or teaching of a Buddha. In this sense, it also means sound, rhythm or vibration.

Shakyamuni Buddha taught that enlightenment is not exclusive. Nichiren created a practical method for making that enlightenment accessible to everyone. As *The Buddha In Your Mirror* states, "Just as Benjamin Franklin's discovery of electricity was not harnessed for practical use until many years later when Thomas Edison invented the light bulb, Shakyamuni's enlightenment was inaccessible for all but a few until Nichiren taught the fundamental practice by which all people could call forth the law of life from within themselves."

Nichiren Buddhism has taken a powerful role in the twentieth and twenty-first centuries through the founding of an organization known as the Soka Gakkai, or Value-Creating Society, which bases itself on the principle of *human revolution*, the profound inner transformation that comes from the practice of Nichiren Buddhism.

Each individual has his or her own specific desires, sufferings or problems (likely a whole list). When we find something important enough that we are not willing to lose it, when we can say that pursuing or keeping this makes us want to be a better person—that is the moment when human revolution begins. And that is why Nichiren taught that desires are not to be eliminated (as many Buddhist schools teach) but are the driving force for the profound inner transformation that is attaining Buddhahood.

The current president of the Soka Gakkai International, Daisaku Ikeda, serves as both teacher and role model of how a transformation of character through Buddhist practice not only brings joy and peace to an individual but creates ripples of change that extend that joy and peace throughout one's environment to the entire world.

THE PRACTICE OF BUDDHISM

Nichiren Buddhism focuses on three basics: faith, practice and study. Faith is to have confidence that Buddhahood exists in all life, including yourself. Practice means chanting the phrase *Nam-myoho-renge-kyo* to the Gohonzon (an object of devotion that was first inscribed by Nichiren Daishonin). Practice also entails sharing with others the Buddhist view of life's dignity and potential for hope, courage and confidence. Through study, Nichiren Buddhists learn about the teaching of Nichiren and the Lotus Sutra.

The incorporation of this threefold practice into one's life initiates and sustains the process of human revolution. This enables us to confront and overcome the very real challenges of daily life. It brings an individual life into harmony with the greater life of the universe awakening the profound potential inherent in life that we experience as wisdom, courage, life force and compassion. Through a consistent practice of Nichiren Buddhism, a person not only gains individual empowerment but also paves the way for humankind to direct its energy toward creating a peaceful and prosperous world.

THE STORIES

What treasures will you find in the pages that follow? You'll read one story after another of challenge, setback, disaster and discouragement met head-on with the compassion, wisdom and courage generated from within by Nichiren Buddhist practice. Story after story of transforming poison into medicine; winter into spring. Story after story of victory over adversity and happiness sculpted from the clay of misery.

Join us for a journey into the lives of ordinary people sharing extraordinary stories. People who have changed their minds and hearts and by doing so have changed the world around them, and the destiny of their lives forever.

ZAN GAUDIOSO
GREG MARTIN

family

The family is a unit where all joys and sorrows are shared among its members. As a result, sadness is more than halved and happiness is more than doubled.
—DAISAKU IKEDA

TO LOVE PEOPLE or to cherish humanity in the abstract is relatively easy. To feel compassion toward real individuals, to love a single human being, is considerably more difficult. Most of us have heard stories of individuals who support worthy social causes, perhaps funding philanthropic organizations or even social activist groups, but whose private lives are characterized by insensitivity, even cruelty to those close to them. By contrast, compassion for humanity in Nichiren Buddhist teachings is not mere idealism—it is something to strive for every day.

One's happiness is based on building a solid inner self. Though Buddhism is a powerful tool for rebuilding inner strength, Buddhist practice is not a solitary activity. Rather, the Buddhist teaching shows that compassionate interaction with others is the most satisfying way to live in society and is, in fact, a virtual prerequisite for enlightenment.

A person of wisdom tries to invigorate and bring out the best in others. The humanism of the Lotus Sutra comes down to treasuring the individual: ourselves, the people around us and all of humanity.

Family relationships hold particular importance. Families are the basis of society, so to build a peaceful society we must first build a happy family. This is why the Soka Gakkai has long stressed the importance of faith for a harmonious family.

In an attempt to keep a marriage together, or sustain a relationship with children, parents or siblings, a willingness to transcend differences is born. It is that willingness that teaches us how to create peace in any relationship where there may once have been disharmony. As the human race is one enormous network of close personal connections— one vast family, in other words—the peace we create in our families spreads out to all.

Le Carré

Mariane Pearl

Adversity gives birth to greatness. The greater challenges and difficulties we face, the greater opportunity we have to grow.

—Daisaku Ikeda

BEHIND THE APARTMENT building where I grew up, on the northeast side of Paris, there was a concrete block that we nicknamed *le carré* or the square. Its real purpose, as far as I can remember, was to provide ventilation for the building. From time to time, hot dusty air would come out of it. When you sat on *le carré*, you would have a view of the building that faced ours, with its tiny windows and parking lot. But for my friends and me, it was the concrete nest of our unfinished selves, a silent observer of our gregarious, insecure teenage lives. It was there that we created love stories and dramas. It was there that we shed tears, shared laughter and spent long boring hours waiting for time to pass.

By the time we were fifteen years old, a lot of us had dropped out of school. The luckiest ones had some direction—they wanted to become musicians. They had a vision for their lives and who they wanted to become. But there we all were hanging out at *le carré*, guys in tight jeans and long curly hair, and some of us girls hiding our bodies behind ample hippie clothes. We felt that only the good-looking girls had a future worth mentioning. We all used slang language created by reversing syllables and introducing Arabic words into our French language.

Most of my friends came from Algeria, Tunisia and Morocco. We also had a few Jewish friends and a couple of Protestants. My brother and I were half Dutch, half Cuban and vaguely atheist. None of us had much faith. My Muslim friends were facing the type of racism that didn't spell its name. It was more of a rampant rejection. If you looked Arabic, or if your name sounded North African, it was more difficult to have high hopes for your life, or to be accepted into French society.

Le carré and the streets surrounding it were our territory and we covered it like a herd. Secretly, we all wished we could fly. We smoked marijuana, and when we were high, even though we were still sitting on that concrete block, we were no longer prisoners of its limitations. Hopes and dreams would be unleashed.

Ben, my best friend, was the oldest son of first-generation immigrants from Algeria. At age seventeen, his father kicked him out of their home, so Ben moved fifty feet away; he moved in with us. My mother had a way of becoming everyone's best friend, and our one-bedroom apartment became a retreat.

My mother, who was widowed at age thirty-eight, had taken on the burden of protecting all of us but was beginning to feel overwhelmed. There were drugs out there and bad guys. Many had parents who were working too hard or had no job at all, who had lost touch with their growing kids. By then, of course, we all dreamt that we could fly to America. It's no wonder that my mother was concerned.

One of the kids who grew up with us, Thierry, called us from downstairs. He was holding his crossbow. He saw my mother's sweet, round face at the window and simply said, "I just killed my father." Thierry had just found out that his father had seduced the girl with whom Thierry had been having a passionate love affair.

My mom took him to the police. It was then that she knew that she could no longer protect us. Things were getting worse all around us.

The Africans had turned to hard drugs. One day, my brother, Satchi, stopped by, hoping to get high. Instead of the usual torpor and lazy atmosphere, he found the stoned dealers surrounding a young woman, a drug addict. She was having sex with all of them in exchange for heroin. The young woman turned her head toward my brother as she was being brutally abused, and my brother knew that he was looking into the face of total despair and self-hatred. For the first time, he was scared for his life.

The next day, he announced that he would be leaving Paris. He and Ben had decided that they were going to move to the south of France, away from the misery we all had started witnessing, to find a job and pursue their dreams.

In Aix en Provence, a small and charming town in the southeast of France, Ben met a young man who played the saxophone and sold circus button pins. Ben and the young man engaged in a conversation about world peace. Ben was attracted like a magnet to this man whose body didn't seem big enough to contain all the energy emanating from this incredible idea: our lives have indeed a purpose, and we all have a mission that is unique and precious.

That same night, Ben went to his first Nichiren Buddhist discussion meeting. He saw people who, instead of criticizing society and being cynical about it, had decided to transform their lives and their environment. They were ordinary people, most of them with ordinary jobs. There were a few Arabs, too, and they had a lot to say. They had hope and the courage to sustain it. And they had positive thoughts that didn't require getting high.

Ben and Satchi started chanting with fervor. Their practice gave them energy and direction. They started to feel stable and more solid with a will of their own. They marveled, as unknown feelings like compassion and hope began to rise in their hearts. They started working hard. "I had seldom felt so happy," recalled Ben. But instead of trying to tackle world peace, a local Buddhist gave my brother and Ben the advice to go back to where they were from and change their own lives.

My mother and I immediately noticed the change in my brother. He looked more exalted, his energy was different and even his voice had changed. My mother was still worried. Satchi would go to the back stairways of our apartment building, and he would hide in the toilet and she thought he had started using the needle. She wept and called on my deceased father to help her from the heavens. The next morning my mother found the courage to stand in front of the toilet door waiting for my brother to come out, but this time there was no smoke escaping from the door. My mother in tears imagined her son sitting on the toilet, holding his arm straight, his fist clenched, looking for a vein. When my brother came out, he was astonished to see our mother so defeated. They sat down on the living room couch and my brother ended her nightmare. "I am a Buddhist," he said triumphantly. He'd been chanting in the bathroom to avoid disturbing us. My mother's relief was so intense that she wept and laughed at the same time, and then she thanked my dad.

Soon after, my brother let go of *le carré* and found his first job at an electric factory. He would live on his motorcycle with his guitar. He was the same young man, yet he was different. He had started making an effort toward his own development and he liked it. His empty rebellion against society turned into a revolution of the self. Buddhist friends were supporting him and harbored no doubts about his ability and eventual victories. He wasn't wasting his life in a cloud of smoke anymore, getting high; instead he had found a solid spiritual ground on which to walk. I followed him on this path, as did my mom and many of my friends.

Ultimately, we were all able to fly away from *le carré* without having to escape ourselves. Nichiren Buddhism provided us with the wings and the direction. We finally understood that we each had a mission that was unique and precious and that our lives would become the stage on which we could accomplish it.

MY HOMELAND
RINAT HAREL

An eye for an eye makes the whole world blind.
—MAHATMA GANDHI

GROWING UP IN ISRAEL I always felt I didn't belong there, and I didn't appreciate the local mentality, which appeared narrow and hostile to me.

For years after I left Israel and moved to the United States, I believed it was the best thing that happened to me. I regretted being born there. I was hoping the rest of my family would follow me here, so together we could build a new life and correct the mistake of ever having anything to do with that dreadful place.

I settled in the United States and made a pretty good life for myself. But much to my dismay, my family never followed me. So I had to keep visiting them there, and things got even worse; the place became increasingly violent with suicide bombers appearing on the streets of Israel starting in the mid–'90s. I was growing to dislike Israel more, if that was even possible.

The cycle of violence got even worse; the second intifada broke out and I, who was visiting there at that precise time, literally drove into a crowd of hundreds of angry Arabs throwing stones.

It was shocking and confusing to me, not only because it was unexpected but also because I was confused. *Are they*

14

really aiming at me? I don't even live here anymore. But on the other hand, I am Israeli.

This second intifada devastated me. I felt there was no hope in sight for a better future in the Middle East. For the rest of that visit I really felt as if the end of the world had arrived; I felt like I was standing on a cliff at the end of a road and under me there was nothing at all. Complete emptiness.

Back in the United States, I started chanting about the violence in the Middle East. It was the only thing that would ease my pain. After a while, it helped me understand that I needed to stop criticizing the two sides and start encouraging peace. My job was to find hope where there was none.

It was after more suicide bombs and their horrific consequences—one of them just around the corner from my parents' house—that I also understood it was time for me to take action, so I decided to initiate dedicated chanting sessions for peace in the Middle East. These sessions would be a time set aside for Buddhists to come together and chant for that specific goal. They took place in the SGI-USA New England Community Center in Waltham, Massachusetts, on Sunday afternoons.

At first, I didn't chant for peace out of love for Israel but out of fear for the safety of the people there and especially for my loved ones. Throughout the years that followed, I have gained a growing hope for peace in that notoriously brutal region. I was inspired by Mahatma Gandhi who had the courage to live optimistically despite what he saw around him.

It was only through practicing Buddhism that I could grow into making a similar choice for myself. And this growth eventually manifested in my relationship with Israel itself. I could see how, instead of feeling horribly impatient with the ways of the place and its people, I had to gradually learn to respect their resilience; through that my criticism would diminish. But I had no doubt that I still didn't belong there.

In January 2004, I went to Israel for another visit. This time I chanted to have the best visit ever. I didn't quite know how exactly I wanted it to manifest, though. I remember the first walk I took the day after my arrival; I was *so* happy to be there, *so* appreciative of everyone and everything that came my way, it was dizzying. I felt none of my old resentment. None! And indeed I had the great visit I had aimed for. I could even imagine myself moving back there in the future. It was difficult for me to leave, when the time came. I felt that a piece of me stayed behind.

I knew that this change of heart must say something about me, since the place sure hadn't improved. It was the war within my own soul that was starting to find some peace. I believe this change in heart, this gift from my Buddhist practice, was the result of my commitment to peace as well as to my personal growth. It is a reflection of my own human revolution through faith. The feeling of freedom from my own negativity that burdened me for so long was my victory, and the poison that was inside me turned into the medicine that I needed. Finally, I know the peace that I have always dreamed of for myself and for a part of the world that I love.

A Fortunate Baby
Eliza Thomas

There is no one to impress, nothing to get, nowhere to rush to, nothing to miss out on. The truth is always there, plain and simple, hiding somewhere near you.
—Elizabeth Lesser

I WAS A "FORTUNE BABY," a child born into the practice of Nichiren Buddhism. By virtue of my discerning taste in parents, my very existence has been fortified by prayer—millions of chanted repetitions of the phrase *Nam-myoho-renge-kyo*. Nam-myoho-renge-kyo was undoubtedly the sound track at the scene of my birth. It was certainly the white noise of my childhood, and when I went off to college, I left the phrase resonating in my wake. As my folks insist, should my sister and I choose to use the power of the practice, there is no end to what we can accomplish.

Asking my parents to define Nam-myoho-renge-kyo can provoke more questions than answers. Practitioners understand it to mean "devotion to the Mystic Law of cause and effect through sound/vibration," and, simply put, my mother and father believe that chanting Nam-myoho-renge-kyo allows them to tap into the "rhythm of the universe." As a child looking for attention, I would do the running man or the robot to the rhythm of the universe, trying to get my parents to crack a smile during their evening prayers.

I grew up on New York City's Lower East Side, where

17

nothing is more unfashionable than enthusiasm. And yet, in my family's apartment at least, enthusiasm was inescapable. My parents had discovered the secret to creating "ultimate happiness" in this lifetime and, naturally, they were excited about it. Even worse, they were determined to share the news with the babysitter, the postman, the supermarket checkout attendant, the crazy cat lady in 3C and every hapless cabbie who gave us a ride. Later, many of these people arrived at our doorstep, tentatively hopeful, drawn by my parents' invitation to stop by for the weekly chance to see their promise of happiness put to the test. It would be hard to imagine a more earnest gathering of strangers, at least in lower Manhattan.

When I was old enough to recognize America's inexhaustible fascination with Eastern religion, I began indulging in the thrill of casually letting it drop among friends that my parents were Buddhist. I enjoyed cultivating the image of my parents doing hip, mystical Buddhist things, like sitting for hours on a *tatami* mat or something, perhaps every now and then turning to give me a contemplative smile. Not quite. The awkward reality of my parents' Buddhist practice—the activities and phone trees, the fervent affirmations, the bagels and cream cheese and effervescence shared at discussion meetings—was, at the time, so dorky it hurt.

The founder and namesake of the practice, Nichiren Daishonin, was a thirteenth-century radical Japanese monk who asserted, in a time of clerical corruption, that every living being had a Buddha nature and could therefore attain enlightenment without the need for an ordained intermediary. Nichiren drew his teachings from the Lotus Sutra. To this day, from New Jersey to Ghana, Nichiren's disciples chant Nam-myoho-renge-kyo, a combination of ancient Chinese and Sanskrit, using the Japanese pronunciation.

Unlike other sects, Nichiren Buddhists embrace their earthly desires as a means to achieve happiness in this lifetime. My parents have an index card next to their altar with an ever-evolving list of their wishes for themselves, their loved ones and the world. By forming a direct alliance between their life-condition and the rhythm of the universe, my parents believe they are harmonizing and strengthening their purest intentions with the life of the universe itself. They call this process "human revolution" and have faith that it will lead them to become absolutely happy and to create world peace by sharing their happiness, person to person.

As Nichiren Buddhists, my parents are members of a global organization, the SGI. In the spirit of engaged Buddhism, members of SGI, one of the world's most ethnically and socially diverse Buddhist groups, base their faith on action. To this end, SGI works closely with a long list of peace, education and environmental protection groups like the Boston Research Center, the Pacific Basin Research Center and the Earth Charter. In addition to their community work, twice a day every day, in their homes and at local community centers, all the world's more than twelve million SGI members sit down and chant in prayer for *kosen-rufu* (the spread of the teachings), understood as the promotion of world peace.

The older I get, the harder it becomes to dismiss the pursuit of world peace as dorky. But *kosen-rufu* is composed of millions of individuals' hopes, desires and intentions, many of which are much easier to make fun of. Because my parents have resolved to see evidence of their prayers wherever they look, they do. In Buddhist terms, this evidence is called "actual proof" or "benefits," and recognizing benefits is a way to maintain an energetic practice.

My parents and I agree that some benefits—such as their successful marriage, the impulsive beginnings of which have now become the stuff of family legend—truly do indicate larger forces at work. My father decided he wanted to get married, so he asked two girls to a Buddhist meeting and proposed to the one who was moved to tears. My mother prudently told him she needed at least a week to decide, dreamed prophetically that my father would be a good match, and now, thirty years later, they are happily married, living in the suburbs, with two kids, two cars, a golden retriever and many reasons to be thankful.

Now that I have passed the quarter-century mark, though, I have less energy to rebel against my parents' resolute benefit-spotting and blessing-counting. Being obstinate and obnoxious was age-appropriate behavior at thirteen, but at twenty-six, and struggling to cobble my way in the world, I am not about to turn up my nose at a dose of self-empowering optimism. Nor am I willing to sacrifice my happiness for the satisfaction of proving my parents wrong. I realize now that there are worse parental vices than enthusiasm. My parents gave me the key to creating positive change in the world, and believe me, when I am driving on a windy, icy mountain road in a snowstorm, I am chanting Nam-myoho-renge-kyo, and I am not smirking.

The first eighteen years of my life were framed by my parents' prayers, and since I left home I have felt buoyed by the power of their determination. As idealistic as it may be, I would not deny that there is something encouraging about being included in my parents' wish to "wrap the world in protective forces." And, admittedly, my life, from my conception on that fateful day at Martha's Vineyard (too rainy for the beach), has been good.

As a fortune baby, cradled in the arms of my parents' focused intent, I had the luxury to take good fortune for granted. But as my adult path becomes less certain, I find myself drawing confidence from the navigation techniques I've inherited, and I am grateful. Undoubtedly, this is a benefit my mother and father have been chanting for all along.

HEALING THE INNOCENCE
JENNIFER R. THOMPKINS

Resentment is like taking poison and
waiting for the other person to die.
—MALACHY MCCOURT

THE DAY I WAS BORN, a Catholic priest was summoned to baptize me and perform my last rites. The doctors felt that my chances for survival were slim. I was born premature at thirty weeks, weighing less than three pounds. Just breathing was difficult, and for three months I stayed in the neonatal intensive care unit.

When I was healthy enough to live at home, a new struggle began just as I overcame the first one: my family life. My earliest memories of my father are of anger and violence toward my mother and later toward me. I do not ever remember peace around him.

As a small child I was nervous to be around him, walking on eggshells. He thought a house should be run with strict rules and that a child should be raised with intimidation, enforced violently if his control was threatened. My environment was conditioning me to be afraid of the world. I was often scared. If I was not perfect, people would not like me or, worse, they might hurt me. I thought my father did not care how I felt or know what I needed or wanted; life revolved around him only. Perfection could not please my father. He was never satisfied.

As I reached puberty, the abuse took another form, sexual abuse. I would dread the days when he would call me into his bedroom and ask me to close the door. I felt helpless and out of control. I would leave my body to find a safe place in my mind until I was actually safe again. At sixteen, the weight of the abuse became overwhelming. It hung over me like a shadow. It was always there, no matter where I went.

My father started laying out plans of what I would do after high school, where I would be going to school and what my major would be. Worst of all he wanted me to live at home to take care of him. This was the last straw; I could not bear the thought of the abuse continuing. I started to have suicidal thoughts. If this was my destiny, I did not want to live to see it through.

Around that time, I befriended an older woman whom I trusted. I told her my horrible secret. She compassionately told me it was not my fault and that she would help me to report the events to Child Protective Services.

My father was arrested, later pleaded guilty and was sentenced to three years in prison. I was so relieved that the nightmare was over, but I was left incredibly wounded inside, unable to trust or to love. I would have years of therapy and healing to do.

Because of all the years of abuse, I did not believe in myself. I did not know how. However, the first healing step came from a seed planted in me as a small child. At the age of ten, I saw my first image of Shakyamuni Buddha on a wall display of world religions at school. I was deeply moved by the photo and the things I read about him. I was a very curious child and that curiosity about Buddhism stayed with me throughout school. Any time I found literature about Buddhism, I read it.

About the age of twenty, I wanted to practice Buddhism but I was unsure where to start. The only Buddhists I had seen were in books of monks and nuns who lived in distant temples and wore robes and shaved their heads.

A student at the community college I was attending placed a flyer about Nichiren Buddhism on the community bulletin board. What I liked about this practice was that I could start doing it exactly where I was in my life. I did not have to do anything special or have any money or status.

I was very eager to learn how to practice. I started attending meetings and learned how to chant and recite the prayers. I chanted to have peace in my heart, presence and clarity of mind and self-esteem. At that time I was unhappy and insecure.

However insecure I was, I hid it under the guise of being a successful student. As a good student, I received rewards from my advisor. But at a self-esteem level, I was surprised that my advisor even noticed I came to school, let alone gave me an award for it.

Fundamentally, I lacked the belief in my own voice; I depended on people's opinions even though I knew this dependency would not lead to happiness. Through chanting, I slowly began to find the center of my own truth. At times I did not like what I found because it meant giving up the negative beliefs I had about myself and letting go of negative relationships. It was a lot of work, but through my consistent efforts, I started to see how precious my life actually was and how valuable I am just because I exist. I began to understand that I am responsible for my own happiness. No one else can make me happy, and I should not be swayed by positive or negative opinions.

Then one day, I got a call from my aunt that challenged me. She called to tell me that my father had a minor stroke and wanted to see me. This brought back many painful memories of him, and I instantly began to cry as soon as I heard the message on my answering machine.

It had been nine years since I had seen my dad. Because of all the chanting I had been doing, I believed I was strong enough to see him again. But on the day I went to see him, things did not go as planned.

I had agreed to see him at the hospital, but I found out that he was to be discharged on the day I was to arrive. Again, this news came via my answering machine. Visiting him in the hospital was one thing, but having to go to his home where there wouldn't be a lot of people around was another. I did not feel safe being alone with him. I was still afraid. I went to bed feeling defeated, questioning everything in my life and why nothing worked out for me. The next morning I woke up remembering SGI President Ikeda's guidance to just keep chanting no matter what happens. I chanted to the Gohonzon and began to cry as I chanted for the courage to now see my dad at his place.

I went to the place he was living, a run-down hotel in San Mateo. When I got to his room I started silently chanting and knocked on the door. The door opened and a figure peered out from the dark room, my dad. He was happy to see me and invited me in. I hesitated but felt it was safe to go inside. Surprisingly, his room was furnished with a bed and a small bookcase. I sat on the edge of the bed and I was overcome by my emotions and I began to cry. I told him how much he hurt me as a child and how I suffered so deeply. He listened attentively and told me how sorry he was and that he loved me. After we talked he invited me to lunch. At lunch I told him about Nichiren Buddhism and taught him how to chant. I explained to him how much it had helped me in my life. I gave him a book *The Buddha in Your Mirror*, hoping that Buddhism might help him the way it had helped me. Maybe it would bring him the same hope and peace that it had given me.

I'm so grateful for my practice of Buddhism. It has allowed me to find the courage to reestablish a relationship with my father even after all the hurt and betrayal. I have come out of this experience not bitter and angry but happy and hopeful. Harboring bitterness does not hurt my father—it only hurts me.

Ultimately, practicing Buddhism has given me a chance to get in touch with my feelings. I realized that I was afraid to feel the actual hurt that was festering in my heart. I ran away from it, doing everything possible not to feel the difficult emotions, because I did not know how deep they went, or where they would take me. I thought that if I really felt the full force of my emotions, I would die or go insane. As a result, I needed validation all of the time to feel that I was OK.

I learned through working with a qualified therapist that I could "ride" the awesome waves of painful emotions and let the tears flow and really feel the fear and hurt in my body. It is really OK to feel. Through chanting and practicing Buddhism, I have felt safe enough to experience the tsunami of hurt; because I know that after the wave breaks, there is a rippling effect of peace.

THE BACKPACK

KATHRYN SPILLANE

What lies behind us and what lies before us are
tiny matters compared to what lies within us.
—RALPH WALDO EMERSON

I REMEMBER THE DAY my friend brought me the story about General Stone Tiger, Li Kuang, a young man who lived in China centuries ago during the Han Dynasty.

The story appears in *The Writings of Nichiren Daishonin*. In the story, Li Kuang is an especially good archer. A tiger kills his mother and he vows to kill the tiger. He hunts all day and as the shadows fall, and night is about to settle in, he sees the tiger. He notches his bow and focuses all his energy on his target. He sinks the arrow up to its feathers, but when he comes close he finds that he has imbedded his arrow into a large rock.

I was impressed by the story but couldn't relate to it because I did not yet have an experience of the impossible becoming possible. My world, however, was about to be stretched beyond my wildest dreams, and Li Kuang's determination was about to become my own.

Shortly after reading this story, my two sons and I traveled to New Mexico to visit family. During our stay we decided to take a trip down to Carlsbad Caverns, about four hours away. It was a lonely, quiet stretch of highway, with flat ground as far as the eye could see. In my rear view mirror, I saw an ambulance approaching with its lights on, so I moved to the side to let it pass. Within a minute I could see the accident, so I told my kids to duck down and stay there, not knowing what might be ahead. As I slowed down and approached the scene, I could see overturned trucks and, much to my horror, the bodies that had been thrown from them. It was a sight that I will never forget. It was obvious that people were dead. A woman's mangled body lay only yards from where my car passed. I have emergency first aid training and thought of stopping, but an ambulance and two police cars were already there. Not wanting my young children to see this sight, I drove on. When we were far enough away, I told my kids that they could sit back up, and they immediately asked what had happened. I was shaking and driving very slowly. I told them that there had been an accident and that people had died. My son, who was only nine at the time, said, "We should chant for the souls of the people who just died, and for their family's peace."

In my shock I had not thought of this, and in a quivering voice, agreed. We chanted Nam-myoho-renge-kyo together for about five minutes. I have never pushed my spiritual beliefs on my children, so their kindness and faith that night really impressed me. We went on to see the Carlsbad Caverns and then returned to Albuquerque. Four days later we were getting ready to return home.

It was a rushed day and the flight was crowded. We didn't get to the Oakland International Airport until ten that night. Both boys were tired; I was tired. With so many pieces of luggage to keep track of, I asked each of them to keep an eye on their own backpacks. We got to the shuttle service to go home, and we were on the freeway when my son asked me, "Where's my backpack?" We looked everywhere. It was just nowhere to be found. He cried. He had all his special stuff from the trip in it, and a few important things from home. I told him I would chant, and I did, right then and there. I chanted that the backpack was already on its way back to us. I was clear in my determination.

The next day I chanted again first thing in the morning, clear and focused. I was sure that the backpack was already coming back to us. It had to. My son checked in with me a few times that day, and I told him that it was already home, we just couldn't see it yet. I took the time to make phone calls to the Oakland Airport and to the shuttle service, but no one had seen the backpack. But I could, in my heart.

Two days passed and I continued to chant. The boys had left for their dad's house and I had kept the same conviction. On the third day I became discouraged. All the hope I had been clinging to was beginning to fade.

That afternoon a good friend came to visit me, to hear about our trip. The first thing out of my mouth was the backpack incident. I told her how my faith in its return was beginning to wane. She encouraged me not to lose hope. I knew she was right. I slammed my hand down on the table and said, "That's it! It's already here, I just can't see it yet!" Adding, a little less fervently that it had to come back, because my kids had to be shown that faith and chanting works. Maybe, though, it was really me who needed the proof.

Less than ten minutes later, my phone rang. I answered it and I heard a woman's quiet voice on the other end of the line asking for me.

She went on to tell me this story. She and her husband had gone on a trip with their nephew, who was only five years old. They got to the Oakland Airport late on the same Saturday night that we were there—only about a half an hour later than us. They asked their nephew if he needed to go to the bathroom and he said "No," so they left the airport. As they were about to get on the freeway, their nephew changed his mind and decided that he did have to go, so they pulled over right there. When kids have to go, they have to go. When they stepped out of their car, lo and behold, they found the entire contents of my son's backpack on the side of the freeway on-ramp. They could have left it there being too rushed and tired to bother picking it up, but instead they picked up each piece they could find, using their flashlight to guide the way.

The woman had found my name and number on a piece of paper. I was speechless and surprised. A warm and wonderful feeling flooded over me as I heard myself thanking her profusely. She took our address and mailed us back everything they had found. Only a few things were missing.

I didn't tell the kids the story until I received the box in the mail. My son was ecstatic about getting his treasures back. I beamed along with him. Not only because he had his things, but also because I got my proof. My chanting had worked.

It wasn't until two weeks later that the lessons from the whole experience started to settle in. I realized that my desire was so pure and so focused that I too had the power to drive an arrow up to the feathers, into solid rock. Or as it happened, to bring a backpack back from the side of a freeway on-ramp. Even to this day when my boys are feeling stuck or hopeless, I remind them that anything is possible through Nichiren Buddhism and the power of chanting. All I have to say is "backpack!" and they instantly know what I mean. They will even get a bit nervous if I say I'm going to chant with "backpack determination," especially if it is something that they don't want to happen. I want to bottle that pure and innocent desire that I had for those few days and draw upon it for all of my life's struggles. Fortunately, my Buddhist friends are around to remind me that that kind of conviction is a state of being; and when I sit in front of the Gohonzon to chant, all I have to do is clear my mind and heart and chant from that calm and determined place.

The other great lesson was that my son got a firsthand experience of cause and effect. He had reached out with love and kindness to the victims of that car accident—strangers he would never meet in this lifetime—and a stranger reached out to him with that same consideration. This whole incident strengthened my faith and gave me courage.

I will never be sure whether it was my determination or my son's wonderful cause that brought the backpack back to us. I think it was a bit of both.

WINTER BECOMES SPRING
DIANA CASTLE

Those who believe in the Lotus Sutra are as if in winter,
but winter always turns to spring.
—NICHIREN DAISHONIN

WHEN I JOINED THE SGI-USA and started practicing Nichiren Buddhism, I experienced many trials in my life, which Buddhism likens to personal winters. These winters would come to test the truth of this amazing practice. I have now experienced many of these winters that never failed to blossom into spring through the great power of this Buddhist practice and chanting Nam-myoho-renge-kyo.

During the first year of my practice, my father died. My husband at the time got another woman pregnant and ended our marriage to marry her; and my agent, who so believed in me and supported my budding Broadway career, closed her agency. These trials in my life would test my relationship to my newfound faith, along with the very fabric of this new family called the SGI-USA.

My first challenge was the death of my father. A holocaust survivor, my father looked to me, his first child born in America, with an eye toward greatness. I would become his victory—a famous singing actress on a first-name basis with the world. At the very moment the phone call came to tell me of his passing, I was chanting to celebrate my first role in a major motion picture. Getting this movie role was

33

what Nichiren Buddhism would call my first conspicuous benefit. I remember how happy I felt to have won it. My father would have been very proud. I continued to chant in appreciation for his life.

The death of my father marked the beginning of my journey toward a new way of living, a deep and profound experience of life based not on winning movie roles but on the kind of movie that I make of my own life—a life that would fundamentally change my erroneous beliefs and pave the way for my own happiness and the happiness of others.

Through every trial, every winter, that I would endure in my life, there would come the spring bringing with it the gift of the winter's lesson. This journey of blossoming we call human revolution.

In the house I grew up in, there were two alternating views of life—the holocaust view and the survivor view. The holocaust view looked out at the world from a mind of annihilation, distrust, isolationism, elitism, powerlessness, victimization, anger, unworthiness and fear. The survivor view saw the world from a mind of deep appreciation for life and everything about living. It embraced a winning mind, poised for a winning life—a mind that recognized the wellspring of the tremendous power within human life to triumph over seemingly insurmountable adversity—a mind that recognized the undaunted courage and unshakable faith of which we, as human beings, are capable.

At that time, I viewed my life from my holocaust mind. But as I chanted every day, studied and attended Buddhist meetings, every obstacle, every challenge became a vehicle for me to challenge this deep fear of life. My practice brought out, like spring emerging from winter, the indomitable survivor spirit that already existed within me.

In the first seven years of my practice, I experienced a lot of what Buddhism calls benefits or good fortune. I was experiencing an abundant springtime, filled with a great deal of good fortune, so much so that my practice slackened. I thought I had everything I needed. I could back off Buddhism for a while. This resulted in a practice that became isolated from others, which ultimately led me back to that old holocaust way of thinking.

It was the compassionate persistence of my friends that always pointed me back to a Buddhist practice for myself *and* others. They encouraged me to participate even when I didn't feel like I had the time or the energy for it. This opened up a vast wellspring of fortune. I got married to my second husband, Steve.

Even though I continued to chant, study and experience positive changes in my life, I went through occasional episodes of isolation from other members. At such times I didn't experience the openness and fresh dynamism that comes from facing deep core challenges of life together with others who chanted. My deep fear of life would reemerge and my gut reactions to my own challenges would revert to the old holocaust mind.

Allegiance to this kind of thinking became an acceptable way of life for me, and after years of practicing Buddhism, I was determined to challenge myself to make deep changes on a core level. I had practiced Buddhism long enough to recognize the truth of my life, and that's where I wanted to live.

With this fresh determination, I returned to practicing Buddhism and studying with others. It was at this time that my husband, Steve, began to chant! We were able to purchase a home and a commercial property that now houses a theater space that we built together. There we create and encourage the power of creativity in the lives of hundreds of people. As SGI President Ikeda once recommended, I was becoming the playwright and leading actor in the story of my own life. This was definitely a reflection of a fundamental change inside me.

Additionally, through the support and guidance of a longtime member, my practice became vibrant and active again. I also found a wonderful group of SGI-USA members. The people in this group are my true fortune. Together we are facing our challenges and limitations. We have been able to learn from and transform the negative tendencies of our past into opportunities that would help build a happier, more fulfilled future. Together we enjoy the present moment as a point of fresh departure. We celebrate each other's victories and support each other in the evolution of our human spirit.

My own family's deep fear of life also began shifting as a reflection of my practice.

My sister had lived most of her life as a manic-depressive person. She attempted suicide many times. Even after thirty years of the best treatment and the best doctors, she was unable to awaken her spirit and challenge her deep fear of life. When I decided that this was no longer an acceptable way for *me* to live, it set the stage for *her* own "springtime" to emerge. She started chanting.

Together, my sister and I courageously face our challenges, recognizing the tremendous power we have within us to triumph over them. Embracing Nichiren Buddhism and chanting has opened our lives like the flowers of spring turning toward the sun. We are more than survivors of life; we have become the creators of our lives.

There is no trial that is more powerful than the truth of Buddhism and there has never been a winter that has failed to become spring.

Maybe, Baby

Anne-Marie Akin

All appears to change when we change.

—Henri Amiel

THROUGH MY PRACTICE of Nichiren Buddhism, I have changed my career path; I am now a musician and teaching artist. I have found the most wonderful partner for my life, built a strong and happy family and surmounted innumerable challenges, both internal and external. I am a person who lives life in a genuine, liberated and courageous way. But I found myself facing an aspect of my life so deeply embedded and painful that I wasn't even aware of its existence until I was (fortunately) forced by circumstances to face it.

The problem began as a result of great joy—after years of talking about it, my partner and I finally took steps to have a child through donor insemination. My partner, Amy, easily conceived. We were, like any set of expectant parents, excited and full of anticipation and we couldn't wait to share the good news with our friends and co-workers. I told all of my friends at The Old Town School of Folk Music, where I am employed. But the majority of my teaching work takes place in a residency program on the west side of Chicago, in a child-care center serving low-income children and families. I found myself unable to tell my colleagues there about the baby.

In my work as a teaching artist, I have observed homophobia, both overt and covert. As any gay person who works with young children will tell you, early childhood education, in any neighborhood, is not an environment where people are typically "out." In the other areas of my life, I had been taking steps to become more and more free, and I suddenly discovered that I had spent the past seven years of my teaching life gradually editing, shrinking and concealing myself, until I had compartmentalized a sort of phony "version" of myself known as Miss Anne-Marie, the music lady. This version did not include many aspects of my self, especially the part of me that is a woman married to another woman. I had worked so hard to come "out" of the closet, only to find myself stuck back in because I had allowed other people's assumptions of me to seem like the truth. Suddenly I was facing "coming out" all over again.

I was faced with a painful dilemma. Here I was, week after week sitting with people who love children and babies, singing with them, looking at pictures of their children and grandchildren, with a heart full of joy knowing that I would soon have a beautiful child of my own; and yet my heart was full of anguish because I couldn't find a way to share my joy. I was longing to tell them. Some of these women were my good friends—except that they knew nothing about my life! How do you come out to people you've known for years?

Amy became more visibly pregnant and my situation became more painful. Total strangers would ask her about her baby, whereas I became more invisible as an expectant parent. Every week I would say to myself, "This week I'm going to tell them." But another week would pass because I couldn't find the words or the courage. I knew that I should chant about it, but it was frankly just too painful for me to even try. I was stuck and miserable at a time when I should have been happy.

One day, about two months before Maya was born, I was sitting in one of the infant rooms finishing a sing-along. In my head I was thinking, *When am I going to tell them?* When one of the caregivers asked me out of the blue, "Anne-Marie, do you ever want to have children?" I thought, *I guess I'm going to tell them now*, so I said, "Well, actually, I'm going to be a mother in September." They raised their eyebrows and looked in mock surprise at my flat belly. Quickly I added, "My partner is a woman, she's pregnant and we are going to raise the baby together."

There was a pause. They didn't look shocked. They didn't look happy. They just completely ignored my statement and one of them said, "So, is anybody gonna barbecue this weekend?" Then they launched into a discussion of their holiday weekend plans. I escaped to the bathroom, where I cried my eyes out.

Weeks went by and I learned that none of the other teachers knew! In a building full of women where everybody knows everything about everybody—no one wanted to "tell my business." I was *stuck* having to tell people myself. It's funny how the universe gives you exactly what you need to grow, but at the time, there was nothing funny about it.

About two weeks before Maya was due—when I would be taking maternity leave—I decided to announce it at the pre-K teachers meeting. I was sick to my stomach. My heart felt heavy with dread, but at the same time I was looking forward to *finally* telling everyone. I was still hoping they might share my joy. After my announcement, the director of the center said loudly, "Congratulations!" trying to set the tone for everyone else. But the majority of faces I looked into reflected back shock, confusion and surprise. A couple of people were very sweet, but my focus was on one teacher who seemed very judgmental, and she was looking around the room for agreement from other co-workers.

I went to the bathroom and cried again. The problem was that I was longing for their acceptance and support—I wanted them to hear my joyful news first and take the news that I am a lesbian in stride. This is not what happened. I was bitter and humiliated.

That evening I chanted to get to the roots of my suffering. As I chanted, I realized that I was carrying deep, heavy shame—a shame I have carried since my own early childhood—a shame so old that I couldn't even name it. Deep down I felt that I was no good, dirty and wrong. The shame I felt about my life was being reflected right back to me by my environment. I sat down and chanted with all my heart to rip shame out of my life by the roots. Every prayer that I chanted felt like I was digging myself out of the dirt. Each day, twice a day, I continued to chant to rid my life of this heavy burden of shame.

The following week the director of the infant toddler programs asked me, "Does my staff know about your baby?" No one had *told* them! I couldn't believe it. She invited me to her meeting, where once again, I would share my news. I was determined that they would meet my happy news with the joy it deserved. After I told them, there was a burst of excited congratulations. They responded exactly as I had always hoped—with pure delight and joy. People started asking me: "How's she doing? Is the baby here yet?"

Our daughter, Mary Maya, now a toddler, comes with me to the center where I do my music. We are able to pay for her to be there. In her classroom their nickname for her is "Little Precious." She is loved and well cared for. One of the teachers, who had once changed the subject by asking if people were going to barbecue, gave me an entire bag of hand-me-down baby clothes. Another teacher brought us a beautiful gift for Maya when she was born. Recently, one teacher cut out an article on gay marriage from the newspaper and saved it for me.

I cannot describe to you the incredible liberation I now experience by being able to be my true self. I am so light and joyful at work. All my relationships have become more genuine. I now eat lunch with the other teachers instead of hiding upstairs. When people ask about my life, I no longer avoid the question or change the subject. I can't believe the heavy burden I carried for so long without being aware of it. I am so deeply appreciative of the struggle I went through to reveal my true self. By doing so I changed my inner state from a state of shame to one of courage, and as a result, my environment changed dramatically.

I continue to chant for pride to replace the shame I felt for the decisions that I have made in my life. I'm determined not to pass those feelings on to my daughter. They say that our children aid us in our Buddhist practice. I am amazed at the changes this tiny life has triggered in me. Even before she was born, she was helping me fulfill my pledge to become absolutely happy and now, I will do the same for her.

THE MIRACLE CURE

JASON HENNINGER

Your miracles are an inside job. Go there to create the
magic that you seek in your life.
—WAYNE DYER

SOMETIMES WE HEAR of people in the direst situations chanting Nam-myoho-renge-kyo and receiving immediate, seemingly miraculous results. Someone wins the lottery, finds out that his or her cancer disappeared after a short time, gets the job offer of a lifetime out of the blue and so on. Such benefits are amazing. You can't help being impressed.

More often though, the benefits of Nichiren Buddhist practice are not big splashy miracles but rather the gradual, steady and reliable improvement of a person's life. Simply put, people just get happier every day. They overcome poor self-esteem, strengthen relationships with loved ones, undo abusive pasts or traumatic losses and more. They learn to face their problems head-on and to be victorious.

Sometimes, though, I find myself hoping for miracles. My son, Morgan, is both gifted and developmentally challenged. He is an affectionate, charming and intense child capable of a brilliance seldom seen in small kids, and simultaneously he has difficulties with tasks and concepts other children handle with ease. Since these difficulties first became apparent, my family has been swept up in a whirlwind of confusing and often contradictory diagnoses, treatments and assessments of his future. The shifting pressure of hopes and fears, theories and evidence, has been a tremendous strain on my wife, daughter and all of Morgan's relatives. Worse still, these difficulties are a constant source of frustration for Morgan.

And so, I've chanted for his mysterious problems to evaporate. I daydream about him suddenly saying, "Look, Daddy, I can do calculus!" or sitting at a piano and playing Chopin with a flurry of precise fingers. I've chanted for his frustration to vanish and be replaced by unfettered genius.

These things are not impossible, and should they occur, I would jump for joy. There's nothing wrong with chanting for a sudden, miraculous change. In some situations, it is exactly what's needed. But wanting a miracle is, in this case, a sign of my own weakness. I say this because the sudden and miraculous improvement of my son would require no change, no work and no improvement on my part. I would sit back and enjoy it and stay the exact same person as before.

Furthermore, when I examine more closely other members' miraculous stories, I find there is always work, always change, always a fundamental challenge preceding the "miracle." The person had to change his or her life on a vital level before the miraculous benefit. The results don't spring out of nowhere.

With that in mind, I have been chanting for more than a mere miracle. I chant to understand how to be the best father for Morgan, how to supply him with the support he needs to triumph. A Buddha is said to possess the virtues of parent, teacher and sovereign. I want to be a Buddha of a father, and the father of a Buddha. Chanting from this perspective, I immediately see many areas wherein I can improve myself.

I find encouragement in these words from SGI President Ikeda: "The good fortune and benefit we create by exerting ourselves in faith will definitely manifest themselves in the lives of our children, grandchildren and all our family. Buddhism is the supreme medicine."

Morgan, I am very happy to report, is improving every day. We're researching ways to help him, to provide him with what he needs; chanting for wisdom, courage and patience and implementing the strategies best suited to him. Perhaps as a result of becoming a better parent, making good choices and working hard for steady improvement throughout my family, I will someday hear him play Chopin—or better yet, his own composition. And I will still jump for joy as everyone talks about what a "miracle" it is.

LIBERTY, THE HORSE STORY
LYNN, ANDY, STEVIE AND GINA RAJECKAS
Written by Lynn Rajeckas

Even though one neither reads nor studies the sutra, chanting the title alone is the source of tremendous good fortune.

—NICHIREN DAISHONIN

I'VE BEEN PRACTICING Nichiren Buddhism since the early 1980s. One of my biggest challenges has been how to encourage my children in faith. After countless hours of chanting for my children's well-being and happiness, I want them to learn early the value of Nichiren Buddhism in their own lives. I want to empower them with Buddhist teachings that show them how they can affect the world, instead of being affected by it.

My children, eight and five years old, and I were heading home from a baseball game. We passed our neighbor's house and they noticed right away that Liberty, our neighbor's horse, was not in his pen. Liberty was a favorite pet of my children. They'd spent hours petting him, feeding him and talking to him. I'm sure they would confide in him and tell him secrets that they didn't want anyone else to know. Needless to say, he was an important part of their young lives and they loved him.

When we went to tell our neighbors, they confirmed our heart-sinking suspicion—Liberty had gone missing. A search team, which included my husband, was quickly formed. Our homes bordered on thousands of open acres; Liberty could be anywhere. My children were so upset. The horse had become like one of the family for them. Jim, Liberty's owner, was distraught. The search team was vigilant, but there was no sign of his precious horse.

My children, seemingly inconsolable at this point, wondered what they could do to help. They were too young to be included in the search team, so they felt inconsequential in the process. I told them how their contribution could be the most valuable, and it would help them feel better too. "We could chant." It was time for all of us to chant together that Liberty would be found and that he would not be hurt. With a sense of mission, my children sat down and chanted Nam-myoho-renge-kyo to the Gohonzon with me. They chanted for fifteen minutes. Now, I can tell you that in the life of a five- and an eight-year-old, chanting for fifteen minutes is like chanting hours for an adult. Their prayers were diligent, sincere and heartfelt. When we were through, my children went to bed. Their hearts were still a bit heavy and they were still worried about Liberty. I'm sure that their prayers had given them a sense that they had done something valuable for their friend; at the very least, it reassured them enough so that they could get to sleep.

At two in the morning, the search for Liberty was called off. Jim decided that he would hire a helicopter the next day to continue the search—he wasn't ready to give up.

A few hours later, with just a moment's rest, my husband, Andy, and I were preparing to chant for Liberty's safe return—it was five in the morning. Before we started, I recounted the story of the children's sincere prayers.

"But I so want to tell them that Liberty's back, when they wake up this morning," I said to Andy. My husband nodded empathetically and then his expression dramatically changed. He was looking toward the room where our altar is, where we chant, and who should be peeking in through the window at us but Liberty.

I immediately ran to wake up the children, while Andy flew next door to get Jim. Needless to say, the children were overjoyed. Their prayers had not only been answered but were delivered straight to their door. The horse was then escorted, in grand style, back to its pen, safe and sound.

Thanks, Liberty, for helping me to show my children actual proof of this wonderful Buddhist practice.

Releasing the Reins

CHRISTINE DUNFORD

If I create from the heart, nearly everything works;
if from the head, almost nothing.
—MARC CHAGALL

WHEN I WAS INTRODUCED to Nichiren Buddhism, I had a profound revelation that the limiting beliefs I'd developed in response to a childhood of poverty were still haunting me. Even though I'd escaped that life and was living successfully in the material sense, I was still operating from a perspective of fear and a need to control—*everything*.

I grew up in a chaotic environment. My father worked sporadically, and when he did it was as a bartender, which was ironic since he was an alcoholic and my mother counted money for a local bus company.

We lived in a tiny three-room apartment in the Bronx, with only a few windows, and the view from every window was the same—a brick wall. The lives of nearly all of my friends were touched, in some way, by alcohol, drugs, physical abuse or sexual abuse.

I can't say that there was a day in my early life that I was not frightened. I was frightened at home, and I was frightened at my Catholic school as well, where it seemed the only way to avoid being hit or humiliated was to strive for perfection. I was a nervous wreck. The only antidote that I could find to my fear and anxiety was ferocious ambition and control.

50

In a sense, it worked for me. I became a straight A student, and I earned a scholarship to Juilliard and became an actress. I made a lot of money, lived in a nice house and had a lot of stuff. I carried a kind of false pride because I believed that I had created my success with *my* efforts, *my* focus, *my* sweat, *my* determination; I was absolutely defined by my struggle and since it seemed to be working for me, I became addicted to it.

When I couldn't be in charge of every aspect of my life, I would become depressed and reclusive, wallowing in shame until I managed to gain control and succeed at something. I could never admit imperfection, and I could never ask anybody for help. It was isolating and exhausting, but anything was better than feeling vulnerable.

The fact that I managed to meet and marry my husband, with whom I developed my first truly intimate relationship, is testimony to his remarkable nature and patience. He supported me through my peaks and valleys, never judging me.

I really thought I had control of my life until I became a mother. Having a child is like some strange science fiction experiment where someone takes your heart—*out* of your body—and puts little legs on it and sends it walking down a busy street.

The love I felt for my child was so overwhelming, it was like nothing I'd ever felt before. It was wonderful. And it was terrifying.

I reached the peak of this excruciating vulnerability when my husband and I learned that our son was going to need surgery. I approached it in my usual fashion, answering my fear with massive amounts of research. I logged hours and hours on the Internet studying his condition. In spite of learning everything there was to learn about his surgery, it was essentially out of my hands, and it was traumatic.

The worst moment of my life was when my two-and-a-half-year old was carried away in the arms of an operating room nurse, crying and screaming and I couldn't do a thing about it.

Although the surgery was successful, and I was grateful that my son was ultimately fine, I felt that I had utterly failed him, failed to protect him. I was quite depressed about it, and becoming increasingly driven to find some way to let go of my fears and need to control.

It was around this time that I was introduced to Nichiren Buddhism. My experience with chanting began with chanting to change, for my son's happiness, and for the well-being of our family.

Shortly thereafter, a friend gave me a copy of *Education for Creative Living,* by Tsunesaburo Makiguchi, founder of the Soka Gakkai. I had some profound realizations. I realized I wasn't going to protect my child by controlling every aspect of his life; and that not protecting him from every hardship didn't mean I was a bad parent. I was able to acknowledge the value in the vulnerability I felt as a parent: it was a natural expression of the deepest love I'd ever felt in my life. I became determined to build the responsibility and character to bear that love and to find more valuable ways to express it.

When I felt overwhelmed by the responsibilities of parenthood, I chanted and chanted, until I finally saw that my challenge as a parent was to learn to live with that much love and that little control.

Even though I'd sought to create a life that would shelter my child and protect him from all the hardships I'd endured, if I was still operating from a place of fear, I was in danger of passing on to him the very same limiting beliefs that I had acquired. And if I did that, then I might as well be raising him in the same ghetto that I had struggled so hard to get away from.

I chanted for the courage to accept the unknown. I chanted to release the need to manipulate everything. Most important, I chanted to be able to accept help from other people.

My first opportunity to see if I was really affecting change came as we prepared for my son's first preschool experience.

The "gradual, loving" approach to separation that had been described at our tour and interview of this particular preschool was nowhere in evidence. My husband was made to feel uneasy about staying, even on the first day. On the second day the director pressured him to leave. My husband once again felt alienated by the director as they locked horns about the separation process. There was a lot of friction and tension, which culminated in the director calling my husband "arrogant."

I felt myself growing angrier and more defensive by the minute. I fought many impulses to confront the director in a hale of anger, then I remembered everything I'd been thinking, reading and learning, and instead of blowing up, I went home and chanted.

Before, I would have "blasted through the brick wall," and in doing so, I would have precluded the possibility— any possibility—of a solution. But now, in spite of my intense feelings of vulnerability and fear, I kept chanting.

The next time my husband took my son to school, the situation had completely changed. The director encouraged him to stay in the lounge for as long as he liked, explaining that the separation process was a delicate one. My husband was stunned and pleased, but didn't know what had caused such a turnaround.

As it turns out, we had friends whose own son had just begun at this preschool. While informing the director of their son's imminent surgery, they told her about our hospital experience.

The director said to my husband, "When a family has already experienced a traumatic separation, it's very important that a school separation be handled sensitively and in a time frame that's comfortable for the child. He needs to be empowered by this situation and to know that he can trust us."

I would never have anticipated this degree of sensitivity and compassion coming from this woman. Had I responded in my traditional manner, she never would have been able to reveal herself in this profoundly humanistic way.

The next day my husband walked my son into his classroom, and my son turned around and said, "Don't you have errands to do? You should go." And that was it. He was happy at school from then on.

All of this happened without me making it happen. It happened without force, without manipulation, and the most important thing was the way my son got to see how this problem resolved.

Somebody once said that ghetto is a state of mind, and what I realized when I started chanting was that even though I had radically changed my external environment in my adulthood, I would never know happiness if I didn't change the landscape of my mind; and the landscape of my mind was absolutely fixed by the limitations of my past. I didn't think anything could change it, until the profound, overwhelming and inspiring love of my child emboldened me to do it and Buddhism showed me how.

LEARNING FROM MY CHILDREN
GREG MARTIN

Consideration equals strength, so the more considerate of others you are, the stronger you will become.
—DAISAKU IKEDA

I WAS CHANTING Nam-myoho-renge-kyo one day when this question pops into my head: *Why are parents of teenagers so angry?* Or, more specifically, why was *I* so angry as the parent of two teens? Demographically, parents of teens must rank near the top of the anger list, I thought, just below disgruntled former postal employees. Why?

I was struck by an idea that I'd remembered from my Buddhist study: people become stuck in anger because they can't be honest with or about themselves. They are caught up in sustaining an illusion about who they are, fearful that the truth—their inadequacies and such—will be exposed for the world to see. They lack the capacity or confidence to let the world see them as they are.

To some extent, with regard to my kids, I got trapped in wearing a mask, a false face. It was the mask of the all-knowing, infallible, wise and compassionate parent. It's a mask one can wear successfully only when our children are little—when they don't know any better. But once they begin to learn the truth of the world, it becomes apparent to them that their parents are not all-knowing, or infallible. I was having trouble dealing with this.

At such times, parents are trying to deceive their children. And whether we like it or not, our children know when we're not being honest with them. They feel hurt and get angry. We may reply in kind and wonder what happened to our little angels.

I remember one episode when one of my children made the bold accusation that: "Well, you don't love me anyway." No parent could hear such a thing without profound disbelief. How could my child ever think such a thing? After all, everything I do is for them.

But as I sat there chanting that day reflecting on this and other episodes, it suddenly became clear to me: Much as I wish it had been otherwise, I had to admit that the accusation was a direct hit. Because at some level, without realizing it, I had been making an unconscious choice to hold onto my mask—choosing to keep up the illusion of unexcelled parenthood—at the expense of my child. I was choosing love of self-image over love for my child. Unbelievable! And profoundly disgusting!

Fortunately, both of my kids survived the experience reasonably well and have grown into truly wonderful and self-confident young adults. If I had realized earlier that it wasn't necessary, or even desirable, to be the perfect parent and that being the ordinary, loving and imperfect human being that I actually am is more than sufficient, then a lot of anger and resultant emotional pain could have been avoided.

So, why was I so angry? One reason, I realized, is because parents are wearing a mask. The kids know it; but the parents don't. As a result, for the masqueraders among us, raising children can become "A Nightmare on Elm Street" rather than an episode of "Father Knows Best."

Since my kids do matter to me—enough for me to want to be a better parent—another important chapter in the ongoing drama of my own human revolution began. The result? Once I realized that my suffering was my problem (not theirs) and began using my Buddhist practice to change myself, my relationships with my kids began to steadily improve. It is as Mahatma Gandhi said: we must be the change we wish to see.

learning and spirituality

A person of success in the true sense is one who
can enjoy a free and unrestrained state of life.
—DAISAKU IKEDA

PEOPLE OFTEN STRUGGLE with deep existential questions such as: "What is the purpose of my life?" "What is my mission?" "And why should I even worry about having a mission or purpose?" "Why not simply enjoy myself?" "Isn't that purpose enough?"

Turns out that it isn't. Our happiness depends on answering the important question of purpose. It is that drive to engage our spiritual nature, that higher self, or Buddha nature. The inclination to have that immanent, eternal, wise part of ourselves play a more dominant role in our lives. It is the spiritual awakening, the fulfillment of the self.

A person without a sense of purpose will be ruled by her or his weaknesses. Obsessions, addictions, emotions and violence will be in control. A person with important things to do finds strength and willpower welling up from deep within and has no problem resisting what others cannot. Purpose is an irresistible force, once again, that spiritual drive. Looking at the social ills of addiction, anger and violence, it seems clear that one root cause is an epidemic of meaninglessness.

That is why one of the effects of this Buddhist practice is to awaken to a sense of meaning and purpose in one's life. Once we, who may have felt insignificant and powerless, begin to feel that we matter and that we can and do make a difference in our lives, the lives of others and indeed in the world, we will live with greater strength and joy. We begin living a life built on wisdom. It is infinitely fulfilling. Grappling with the question of one's mission is inseparable from the struggle for one's happiness.

But what, then, is one's mission? The common concern is high on the list of the "big questions" of life. When we embark on that spiritual journey, we will begin to answer those questions. Once, when asked about this by a young person, SGI President Ikeda responded that it doesn't have to be anything glamorous or extraordinary—reiterating that ordinary people living ordinary lives are important, too. He said, simply, your mission is to "Climb the mountain in front of you."

Whatever problem, difficulty or mountain we currently face—overcome it, solve it, climb it. And when we get to the top of that mountain we will look out and see new peaks, new mountains to climb. And new ones after that. We never reach a plateau of "no problems." There is no end to our vast learning so we continue to climb throughout our lives.

My Name Is Cary

Cary Hungerford

Courage is the price life exacts for granting peace.
—Amelia Earhart

I HAVE BEEN SUFFERING with deep depression for as long as I can remember, and I'm still a teenager. It wasn't until the last five or six years that my depression increased, seemingly triggered by my difficulty in maintaining relationships with friends. I continually gravitated toward crowds of people who, I didn't realize, were in their *own* states of depression. I would then become uncomfortable, internalize what they did and said and ultimately isolate myself. This was followed by a deeper and deeper depression and self-hate.

When my mom discovered that I was seriously considering suicide, we sought professional help. My mom told me to chant every day as if my life depended on it. I had no choice but to try because my life did depend on it.

I hated my school. I was convinced that I would never escape my misery, so I chanted to find a better school. I heard about a private school through friends, and I decided I'd start there despite the impossibility of being able to afford it. I was immediately accepted into this very expensive college prep school on full scholarship when the director discovered that, on my own, I was reading *Dreaming War* by Gore Vidal, one of her favorite authors. That would be just one of many such coincidences that would happen.

In the first week at my new school, I met the ideal buddies. Life was looking better, I was doing well in school and I was partying with my new friends. But after only a short while, I started feeling anxious again, and while my friends were getting high just to party, I noticed that I needed to get high just to be comfortable in my own skin. I became powerless over my addiction. I was unable to manage my life at home or away. Things escalated rapidly and I came crashing down, this time to a mental hospital where I was on a twenty-four-hour suicide watch.

I began to understand that the suffering was inside me—my surroundings weren't the cause of my suffering; rather my sufferings were mirrored in my surroundings. According to Nichiren Buddhism, our lives and our environment are inseparable. My life was one of self-loathing. This is a state known as hell. Even though I found "better" people, places and things, it was only a matter of time before the "new" place became hell for me too. My environment continued to reflect back to me all the hate I had for myself. I needed to change *inside*. I finally chanted to become happy.

I was discouraged, but my mom kept telling me that somehow, even through the mud that I was in, I could create value. In Buddhism, this is called "changing poison into medicine." Sure enough, when I look back now, that terrible week and the following months of rehab and therapy have actually changed the course of my life.

Since then, I have been chanting every day, and as I begin to accept and love myself as I am, my life is attracting much different circumstances. Somehow, I was able to get into a very expensive rehabilitation facility that ordinarily is not covered by insurance, but they made an exception for me. Then just as the insurance coverage ran out, my favorite counselor actually started his own program. This was successful financial outcome Number Two; my school scholarship being Number One.

What I had originally chanted for—the ideal assortment of people in my life—well, I never would have figured that it would take such a journey for me to find them, but I have. They are people who know and love me, whom I respect and identify with and love.

I am back in school, which is also remarkable based on the wreckage I had caused, and I'm carrying a full load of advanced placement classes.

Where I had often chosen to be home alone and miserable before, I am now "never home" (according to my mom) because my life is full of great people whom I love to be around. But most important, I now love to be around myself.

I don't use any substances to hide my pain any more. I have chosen self-love and approval instead. I continue to chant and I volunteer for my local SGI-USA organization so that I may help other people practice to find their own peace.

I am thinking about my future now, a future that did not exist before.

CARY'S MOM

KATE HUNGERFORD

What is most needed in this ever more confusing world
is the kind of dialogue that, based upon mutual trust
and respect, is capable of transcending any
differences among people.

—DAISAKU IKEDA

M Y SON, CARY, came close to committing suicide. Our stories, by no accident, dovetail and have served to change our own lives, our own destinies and our family's habitual and destructive course.

I was born in a federal housing project in Philadelphia. My childhood was full of constant and inexplicable suffering and tragedy. I tried to rise above my poor dysfunctional family by achieving honors at school. I never brought friends home—it was too embarrassing. The first opportunity I had, I moved three thousand miles away and started my own separate, better life.

Imagine my disappointment when at thirty-four, married to a successful director, with my firstborn child and my stylish friends, I found myself fighting addiction and domestic violence. Thus began my journey along the same path of destructive behavior that was indicative of our family. Nothing had changed within my own life, so I had no choice but to follow my family's path. It was as certain as was our DNA for brown eyes.

My Nichiren Buddhist practice has changed the trajectory of my life by teaching me how to create value with the circumstances I encounter, instead of trying to escape them, and my life looks very different today. But when I discovered my sixteen-year-old son's intention to commit suicide, it seemed like the family's propensity for deep-seated unhappiness and self-destruction was repeating itself. The terrible memories came flooding back; my youngest brother's battle with manic depression, the mental hospitals, the medication nightmare and finally, his suicide.

Surely I had changed that negative familial pattern by now? But chant though I did, we had started down that same awful road. My outspoken distrust of the drug companies and the medical industry, in general, made it worse. I believed that drugging kids was almost criminal, and I felt that people who did so were just ignorant. But even though we tried every alternative form of healthcare and supplement therapy, the situation escalated until my son had to be put on antidepressants. I put that first pill in my kid's mouth, and I cried and chanted most of the night. At some point, I started thinking about all the parents who had to do the same thing.

Buddhism postulates that the exact position you find yourself in holds the key to your growth. I don't think there was another situation in the universe that could have widened my perspective on this subject. My strong opinions about so many things were based only on my knowledge, not compassion. And my decisions frequently came with a sense of intolerance. My respect for diversity, when you got right down to it, was more along the lines of, "I'll give you all the time you need until you see it my way." It was hardly the kind of understanding that melts hearts.

I thought about SGI President Ikeda's broad embrace of people who, on the surface, professed ideologies that clashed with his own, and yet they seemed always to be open to his thoughts. What was it that opened doors for him that others couldn't enter? He has met with world leaders and has embraced a campaign for peace in this world. Then I realized that it all boils down to his compassion for people's circumstances, because it's compassion that opens the door to understanding, that turns knowledge into wisdom and ultimately creates peace in one's own life and in the world.

I knew at that moment that everything came from my ability to embrace and understand, instead of resisting and repelling. Through it all, I was even able to extend compassion to the drug companies, appreciating them for their ability to help and serve people—especially in their times of crises.

My son did *not* repeat our family's destiny, its karma; he transformed it through his chanting. And I am certain it was our family karma. Of the hundreds of possible drugs on the market today, my son is on the very same medication that my brother was taking when he decided to end his life, but Carey is thriving and living a better life.

Unlimited Self-Esteem

Amy Schor Ferris

*The greatest discovery of any generation is that a
human being can alter his life by altering
his attitudes of mind.*
—William James

IT WOULD CREEP UP on me at the most inopportune
times. While I was driving my car, walking down the
street, having a romantic dinner with my husband, it would
start to churn away; slowly but surely, that little tiny voice
that says, "I'm not good enough," "It's impossible," "Who
are you kidding?"

That little voice got louder with each step I took, with
each road I traveled, with each kiss my husband planted on
my lips; the unending voice of doom.

For many years that voice—that insidious voice—had
complete control over me. It felt like an unwanted friend.
You know the type I'm talking about—someone who calls
incessantly, who never asks how you are but just rattles on
and on and drains you of all your energy. You try to say, "I
can't talk now," but they don't hear a word you say.
Instead, they act as if they are entitled to your time and
space. That's what my self-doubt and low self-esteem began
to feel like—an unwanted friend who, no matter what I did,
just wouldn't go away.

I equated this lack of self-esteem with all the clothes

hanging in my closet that no longer fit. Every day I would open my closet and see with my own two eyes what I no longer needed or wanted, what no longer fit, and yet, resisting, deeply afraid of giving away anything, I would simply close the closet door and act as if it didn't exist. On days when my self-esteem rose above sea level, I fantasized about tossing everything, having all this space to buy sassy new clothing and of course, in that fantasy world, everything was in its place, all matching hangers, shoes lined up on the floor and always something fabulous to wear. To put it another way, it would be uncluttered. Those fearless fantasies came and went in a snap.

Until one day, I was walking down the street, sipping a hot and foamy cappuccino, when a voice intruded: *You're never going to fulfill this dream. It's utterly impossible. You're not good enough; you can't do this. It'll never happen.* I stopped dead in my tracks and thought to myself, *This negativity, this self-loathing is cluttering my heart.* I decided right then and there to tackle it, from the inside out.

While self-doubt and low self-esteem have been etched inside me my entire lifetime, I am unbelievably fortunate in so many other ways. I realize on the most fundamental level that life is, in fact, a journey, and only truly when we are ready to conquer something, overcome something or accomplish something does the opportunity present itself. I now see the value of letting things unfold and am ready to let this issue of self-doubt unfold.

I reviewed my entire life. Through much tear-stained chanting, as I dug deep inside I saw, to my amazement, a continuing thread of self-doubt, a deep lack of self-confidence that unraveled from childhood to adolescence to womanhood. Those feelings of not being good enough, not belonging—the need to please, the need to be loved and liked, the need to feel important, to feel wanted, to be accepted, to be validated, to be approved of, had knotted for forty-six years.

For years and years, I would think, *If I just had this I would be happy, if I just had that I would be happy.* Well, I was surrounded by "this and that" and still felt unworthy, undeserving and, more importantly, unhappy. What struck me was that despite these feelings of unworthiness, I had fulfilled my dream—a joyful, loving marriage, a successful career as a writer, financial security, two beautiful homes, great friends—and yet I still felt that I wasn't good enough. I decided it wasn't about filling my life with more "stuff," it was about getting to the root of my suffering and pain. Nichiren Buddhism teaches that the human revolution of one person revolutionizes and transforms the environment. That seemed like a perfect, albeit difficult, place to start: to change how I feel about myself.

If pain and suffering were inside me, well, then it was up to me to change my opinion of myself. Then came the defining moment in my life. I was mere steps from accomplishing another huge goal. I was so close. The pity party I was throwing for myself was in full gear. I was most definitely scared and filled with tremendous doubt. I decided it was time to seek some encouragement, some advice. I went to see a Buddhist friend.

My eyes filled with tears as I gave him a blow-by-blow account of all the raw details of my life—the obstacles and challenges, doubts and fears that were consuming me. He listened patiently as it all came tumbling out of me. Then he took my hand and said, "Please chant to be a woman of unlimited self-esteem." It sounded so poetic. I began chanting that way—to be a woman of unlimited self-esteem. Every fear, every doubt, every single feeling came to the surface, right up to my nerve-endings. I had two choices, either give in to this self-slander and self-doubt or challenge and transform these feelings lodged in my soul. I chose to challenge myself.

To be honest, it felt like "do or die." For two weeks, I engaged in a battle, an internal battle. There were days when all I could do was cry, feeling sorry for myself. There were days when I was amazed at my determination, feeling proud of myself. There were days when I felt nothing. There were days when I felt powerful. There were days when I felt shame and guilt, and there were days when I felt appreciation; I felt humble. There were days when I still felt like a sham, and days when I felt authentic. And there were days when I didn't think I could go another inch.

Then, after two weeks of chanting, I felt a sudden shift deep inside me. It dawned on me that I had viewed my doubt as an effect rather than the cause. It became clear that the environment was merely reflecting how I felt about myself. For so many years, my thought pattern was, *She doesn't like my work, so I guess it's not good*, or *He is saying it can't happen, it's impossible, so I should just give up.*

I allowed my environment to choose my life, to decide the outcome. I never once thought the negativity that was coming at me was a reflection of how I truly felt about myself.

The minute I understood that in my soul, it was liberating. I was chanting Nam-myoho-renge-kyo and felt a surge of energy. My back straightened up, my palms pressed firmly together, and I felt, deeply felt, worthy of respect. From that moment on, I chanted with a profound sense of appreciation for my life. That's when I truly understood what self-esteem isn't, and I finally understood with my life what it is.

Self-esteem is courage, the courage of one's convictions. It is confidence, the confidence to stand up and own your dreams, every bit of them. It is respect, respecting each and every feeling—both negative and positive—that may come up in the process of fulfilling that dream. It is honoring one's life, honoring the struggle, the challenge, the ability to take one more step on a road that feels unbelievably long and winding, and it is faith, from the time we make up our minds to accomplish something to seeing the result of that determination. It is that in-between time, when the doubt and self-loathing and the fear creep in, all the dreams feel as if they are falling or slipping away—that's when we get to see what we're made of; that's when we reveal our own inner strength and limitless potential. That's when I realized what it means to be a woman of unlimited self-esteem.

Armed with this new realization resulting from my prayer, I determined that I would take full responsibility for my own happiness and create the greatest victory through my own unyielding actions. SGI President Ikeda states that once our determination changes, everything moves in the direction we desire. The actual proof that manifested from this newfound determination was quite outstanding, but the struggle to win over myself was far more astonishing— and will no doubt last a lifetime.

COMING OUT

DANIEL HALL

Not everything that is faced can be changed,
but nothing can be changed until it is faced.
—JAMES ARTHUR BALDWIN

THE PERSON I AM today is not the person I was a few years ago. Today, I am happier than I have ever been in my entire life and my spirit absolutely overflows with determination and optimism toward the future. Without a shadow of a doubt, my present state of being is a direct result of my Nichiren Buddhist practice. However, I didn't always practice Nichiren Buddhism and my life wasn't always this way.

For virtually my entire life, I had been completely consumed by my own personal hell. Ever since I was thirteen years old, I knew I was gay. As I grew up, I constantly heard the word *gay* thrown around as an insult by my friends and even by members of my family. I remember, as a kid, watching television and feeling absolutely terrified as political and religious leaders totally bashed gay people, calling them abominations or evil deviants that deserved to be hated. Because of experiences like these, I hid this part of my life, lived in constant fear of rejection and hatred, and my life degenerated into a pathetic state of hopelessness that I could ever be myself, be happy or find true love. Worst of all, I had given up hope that I would ever experience unconditional love from, and deep relationships with, my friends and family. Hiding this part of my life created a horrible isolating distance between the people I loved and myself. I hated my life, and suicidal thoughts constantly cut into my mind. I really suffered, and because I was too afraid to face this dilemma, my suffering only grew worse.

At my lowest point, the stress and depression caused by keeping that secret and constantly living in fear had taken a serious toll on my health. I developed insomnia and was diagnosed with chronic fatigue syndrome that was so severe at times that I wasn't able to read a single sentence in a book or magazine. I stopped eating, lost weight and developed a triple bacterial infection in my sinuses that caused a hearing loss that would require surgery to repair. I was dying, and I knew it.

I felt so ashamed that I didn't have the courage to fight. Then, in what seemed like my darkest moment, something amazing happened. Like a beacon of hope in my mind, I remembered the Buddhist practice I had been born into. I had quit because I didn't really believe that chanting did anything. Although I was still skeptical, I honestly thought I would die if I didn't do something. So I chanted. I chanted diligently. I chanted like it was a matter of survival, because it was.

I immediately felt better and more hopeful. Eventually, I noticed that a surge of confidence and hope would well up from within me every single time I chanted. After only three months of continuous and sincere chanting, and after a veritable lifetime of living in fear, I had somehow managed to develop the courage to completely come out to my friends and family.

You might be wondering what their reactions were. My dad told me that he was very proud of me and soon after, we marched together with an SGI-USA Buddhist group in the Los Angeles Gay Pride Parade. My mom told me that she didn't care and that I was her son and she would always love me. My sister, the first person I opened up to, gave me her full love and support. And my friends, though shocked and skeptical at first, gave me their full love and support and only wished I had told them sooner. My insomnia and infections disappeared, and though I still battle fatigue, I am overcoming it. Because of Buddhism, my life has undergone a complete revolution. I went from being hopeless and suicidal to being so incredibly grateful for my wonderful life, full of such unconditional love from the people who mean so much to me.

I felt like I had been given a second chance to make my life worth living. I was determined to give back and contribute where I could and create value with my life. I was inspired by Nichiren Buddhism. Although I was still very ill, my energy and lust for life were exploding and I had never felt happier.

Around the same time, I participated in the Orange County AIDS Walk—something I never would have done had I not come out of the closet. During the opening ceremonies, I heard the mayor of Irvine give a short speech describing his efforts to promote diversity and tolerance within the city. I had never heard any city official, let alone a mayor, speak like that.

After his speech, I ran up to him, shook his hand and told

him how much I appreciated what he had said. We chatted a bit more and eventually, he suggested that I call his secretary and set up an appointment to talk further with him.

When I went to City Hall, I was able to tell him about the Victory Over Violence committee for the SGI-USA Orange County Summer Festival I was involved in. I told him about my desire to bring VOV outreach workshops into the community. To my surprise and delight, he was interested in the idea and suggested that I put together a proposal describing what I wanted to do with VOV in the city. Then he said I had one week to do it. I thought to myself, *Wow! What a great opportunity to create a really positive change in Irvine.* So even though I had never done anything like this in my entire life and hadn't the slightest clue where to begin, I said, "Absolutely."

Over the next five days, I frantically contacted every Buddhist friend I could find for advice on how to create this proposal, and I chanted. I chanted at home, at work, in the car, in the shower, in between bites of food—every waking moment—with the single-minded focus that I would succeed in creating a powerful and viable proposal. Then, after five days, it was done.

The day after the mayor received it, he called to tell me how impressed he was and that I should come in for a second meeting.

At our second meeting, not only did the mayor inform me of his intention to attend and speak at our SGI-USA festival, he also declared the day "Victory Over Violence Day" and authorized an official letter recognizing our efforts. He also voiced his desire to visit Soka University of America (an independent liberal arts university founded on the Buddhist principles of peace, human rights and the sanctity of life), read SGI President Ikeda's peace proposal, and best of all, offered me a job to work as his executive assistant.

As his assistant, I achieved my goal of doing work that would make a positive contribution to society. He gave me such wonderful projects as an outreach to universities throughout Orange County including Soka University, organizing the first city-sponsored multicultural dialogue, organizing voter registration drives and an all-day forum on child and elder poverty.

I felt very appreciative and inspired by the power of Nichiren Buddhism in my life. Many positive changes took place for me when I decided to practice Buddhism, not just because I was raised with it but because my life was calling for it. Both my mom and sister, who were suffering with their own problems, started to chant again.

What I learned from this experience is that Nichiren Buddhism is powerful. It revolutionizes lives. I have gone from contemplating suicide to helping my family and making a difference in society.

I am grateful for my struggles because they have given me my life, my passions and my dreams. I've learned that my struggle is my joy. By coming out, I had to go deep within and find self-love and respect in order to extend it outward, and that makes me very grateful for my Buddhist practice—and that makes me very happy.

PROTECTED

GALE HULL

A light for one is a light for a hundred.
—THE TALMUD

I WAS A BUS DRIVER for the Chicago Transit Authority. One summer evening I was nearly finished with my route, working California Avenue. Running times generally increase once in the evening, at rush hour. When rush hour is over, there are fewer riders for the rest of the night.

This was the case this particular evening. As I was turning around at the bus terminal to head back southbound after rush hour, I was running a little bit behind schedule so I really had to move down the street.

As I started out, I picked up three teenage girls who sat in the back of the bus. As they boarded, I noticed that I had three green lights for about the next five streets. I knew I could get through them all safely, so I proceeded with that in mind.

When I approached Washington Boulevard, a three-lane, one-way street, I looked over to my left and to my shock, I saw a car full of passengers running the red light. They were headed straight for me! From my experience as a driver, I knew that this vehicle was going at least forty miles per hour, and the driver probably never noticed the red light because he didn't even attempt to slow down.

When they got closer to me, I could see the horror on their faces. My heart sank as my gut tightened and cringed.

Then, for what seemed like an eternity, all I could hear was the loudest sound of tires and brakes screeching. I was waiting for the dreadful boom of the collision, but none came! I felt something very lightly brush across the rear bumper of the bus. As I looked to my right, their vehicle was continuing down the street. Could it be possible? Could we really have missed each other? That was just physically impossible!

My three young passengers were thrown to the floor when I hit the brakes. I asked if everyone was OK, and then I apologized for the rough ride. They said they were all fine but a bit stunned. They could tell that a major catastrophe had just been avoided.

The girls got off at their stop, and I was alone on my bus for the next couple miles, still shocked and stunned by what had just happened. It was amazing that I didn't collide with that car. I should have, by all rights, been on the news that night as a result of a terrible, perhaps fatal, accident.

I will eternally be grateful to this wonderful Buddhist practice that daily helps me with problems by teaching me how to fundamentally change my life, to live my best and makes me feel fulfilled, but I will never again take for granted the unseen protection that surrounds me because of it. When I recite my morning and evening prayers, I align with the protective forces of nature.

And though they may never know it, there are some parents out there who also received the blessings of Nichiren Buddhism when their children returned safely to their homes that night.

THE WISE LOTUS

BIANCA GREENE

If you cross one more mountain of hardships, you will
find indestructible happiness then and there.

—JOSEI TODA

I SPENT MY CHILDHOOD years surrounded by wealth
and all the advantages it brings: proper English nannies,
travel, private schools, my own pony—in short, anything
money could buy. The icing on the cake was a close-knit
family; I was living the American dream at the age of six.
Two years later what had taken my parents years to build
began to rapidly unravel. My so-called perfect life came to a
crashing halt. Overnight, I was living in a contrasting reality,
the polar opposite of everything I had come to know.

The FBI came knocking at our door taking my father off
to a maximum-security federal prison. That was the last
time I was to see him for almost a year before my mom was
able to set up visitation rights. Those visits would continue
during the next four years.

I was drawn into a vortex of shame, insecurity, hopelessness and fear. It was beyond my comprehension to grasp
the extreme upheaval that would eventually culminate in
my parents' divorce. My mother, with her indomitable
British spirit, was the engine that moved my sisters and me
to safety. Our family motto became "adversity into empowerment." I was born into a family that practices Nichiren

81

Buddhism, a faith that I still maintain today and will throughout my life.

Through all this turmoil having an older sister, A.J., as well a twin sister, Sam, was comforting, but this too presented its own challenges. It seemed that I was always running to catch up to them. A.J. was the perpetual "Perfect Kid" and Sam has always come in first at everything. She even beat me into this world by a minute and forty-seven seconds!

I made the decision to personalize our family motto. I took my "runner-up" sibling status and used it as fuel for my own empowerment. First, I became determined to change my average grades into honor roll material. I hit the ground running. Sacrificing my sixth and seventh grade summer vacations, I enrolled in a special program. Although I did not get extra credit for it in school, it served to enrich my life and it prepared me for future academic and artistic challenges.

The following summer, I persevered and successfully completed the course. Since then I have continuously made the honor roll. It would be the beginning of me forging my own unique path. I became successful in taking myself out of the shadows of my sisters' accomplishments. What I gained most out of my efforts, however, was a real sense of pride knowing that I was able to reach my full potential both personally and academically. It resulted in raising my self-esteem and confidence.

The next thing I wanted to do was to polish my character as I continued this journey on the road to my development.

My newfound attributes were gained by overcoming my adversities, whetting my appetite to personalize my Buddhist practice and make it real in my own life as opposed to it being the background religion that I was born into.

I had always enjoyed all aspects of participating in the SGI-USA, so I became more involved. I was immediately given a role of responsibility in our youth group. I was to help the kids in our group direct their efforts toward overcoming difficulties in their own personal lives and at the same time doing it for myself. This is how my true mission came into focus.

My Buddhist practice helped me deal with the pain of those dreaded Saturday morning prison visits with my father and the circumstances that led up to his imprisonment. It has helped me understand, accept and overcome my feelings of loss, anger, resentment and being a victim—there's no empowerment in that stance, that's for sure. The loss of what was once all so perfect has helped me delve deep into my own life and find my own strength. It has served to help lay down deep roots of faith so that I can be certain that no matter what the future may bring, I will be ready.

I have a newfound sense of self-esteem, pride and faith. As a result, I am in a position to reach out to others who might be going through the same thing in order to help them. I understand. I have been there. From this point I am prepared to forge a future filled with possibilities because I have learned, through faith and a strong network of family and friends, that nothing is impossible. My adversity has indeed become my empowerment.

Peaceful Warrior Story

Steve Lovold

Written by Zan Gaudioso

*We must learn to live together as brothers
or perish together as fools.*
—Martin Luther King Jr.

W E ALL HEARD the order to open fire, expend all ammunition. We were under a UN-sanctioned cease-fire and everyone knew it, yet the chain of command was ordering our unit to "fight to the death." We were just outside the city of Al-Basrah, in Iraq, when we proceeded to carry out the orders. Apparently, there were reports of Iraqi Republican Guards hiding out there. On that day we killed twenty-one hundred people—women, children, old men and Iraqi soldiers. It was never clear in a subsequent investigation whether those soldiers were armed or simply surrendering. How was I going to live the rest of my life with this nightmare?

I was nineteen years old when I volunteered for the military. I was bored. In school I had excelled in art and drafting. I was good at it, but it wasn't enough to keep me engaged. I had been studying martial arts since I was ten. I was tough. That's what I thought it meant to be a man.

The fights I got into protected the underdog until I started abusing drugs and alcohol. When I turned sixteen things changed. I learned just how strong I was. One day when my stepfather kept hitting and hitting me, I just snapped and hit him back. I clocked him so hard that I sent him reeling with just one blow. It was then that I knew that I could stand up for myself, and I went looking for fights. Signing up for the military just made sense.

When our country became involved in pre-operations for Operation Desert Shield, I became part of an advance party of the Eighteenth Airborne Corps that was sent to the Persian Gulf after Iraq had invaded Kuwait. We would be among the first combatants in the theater.

At one point when I was in Saudi Arabia guarding the perimeter of the Iraqi border, a truck was fast approaching. The truck looked like it could pose a possible terrorist threat. From a distance though, it looked as if two boys were in it. I knew if I laid down a line of fire that the bullets could ricochet and possibly kill one of the kids. Against orders I jumped out of position, flopped belly down on the road and pointed my weapon right at the driver. Still they didn't stop. I had only a split second to decide if I would fire. As my finger pulled the slack on the trigger, the truck slowed to a stop and began to turn around. It turned out that it was just a couple of Bedouin kids out joyriding after all. With my heart still racing, I began to take stock of my situation for the first time.

In Iraq I was OK with the combat situations. I was just doing my job and following orders. What I didn't realize is that being there in that violent and surreal world—where some soldiers were hanging the severed hands and arms of their victims in their vehicles—was like sticking your finger in boiling water. At first you don't feel it, but eventually the pain kicks in. Sure enough, the pain from the horror I was living was about to kick in for me.

When I joined the army I was young and impressionable, but I played the game well. By the time I left I had earned close to twenty medals. I soon began to feel, however, that I was just a pawn for old men in armchairs playing with our lives. I believe I participated in events that went against the Geneva Convention. It was even possible that I was part of a war crime.

When I got home, I had gained a bit of notoriety because of articles that appeared in the local papers. As one of the initial combatants from Los Angeles sent to the Persian Gulf, I was asked to speak at Christian churches and appear at special events. I was being treated like a hero in a romanticized version of war. I didn't feel like a hero. There was nothing romantic about it, and I was in pain.

When the depression got so bad that I couldn't stand it anymore, I went to the Veterans Administration for help. They told me that I was the first person to come back from the Middle East with emotional problems. Later I learned that they were telling everyone the same thing. It was their pat answer. The only way I could cope was to drink and self-medicate.

I felt betrayed. I felt lost. I felt alone. I started having flashbacks of my experiences and lost hope. I accumulated so many DUIs that I was arrested and sent to prison. The Veterans Administration finally diagnosed me with post-traumatic stress disorder and prescribed psychiatric meds for me. Because I was on medication, however, I was sent to a maximum-security facility.

I was in prison for one year with serious criminals where the average sentence was fifteen years. On the upside, I met a Buddhist monk who taught me meditation, and I joined Alcoholics Anonymous. I was still a prisoner though, not just in my physical environment but also in my head.

When I got out I didn't have to worry about being a hero any longer. I was now an ex-con. I started drinking again and hanging out with drug dealers and gang members who tried to convince me that working for them was my only choice. Since I was now a felon, I believed them.

But I knew that if I didn't stop drinking I would die; and yet I was just as terrified to stop as I was to die. Eventually, I stopped drinking. I also stopped hanging out with criminals.

I was working some construction jobs and doing some deep sea diving, but money was tight. Then a friend gave me the number of a private contractor. He offered me a job that would pay thirty-five thousand dollars a month. The catch? It was as a security agent in Iraq. I told him I would have to think about it. I felt trapped. The money was the only reason I considered it.

I quickly got my answer. The thought of going back to Iraq made me a basket case mentally, emotionally and physically. Because I was sober, there was nothing between my pain and me. I started having nightmares, lost my appetite and couldn't sleep. I didn't have a good grasp on reality because I was so sleep deprived. If I heard a loud noise I would react as if someone was firing a weapon. I knew I couldn't go back.

I got more counseling and tried to be more "social" in order to reconnect with reality and with people. I was such an emotional wreck that I couldn't even concentrate enough to hold down a job. I tried yoga and mediation, but nothing really helped. Then a friend introduced me to Nichiren Buddhism. While I was skeptical, I was willing to try anything. I started chanting.

Immediately I got results. I started to sleep and eat. For the first time in years I started to experience a sense of peace. I continued to practice Buddhism and I continued to get relief. I noticed that my life was changing because I was attracting people who were emotionally healthy. I realized they were reflecting the changes in me. I was becoming whole again. I was emerging from the darkness of my self-imposed prison.

Recently, I have been able to return to school because I can concentrate again. I'm working on getting my college degree. I am studying and excelling as a business major. Also, my creative side has resurfaced. I am grateful to see that through it all my talent as an artist remains intact. I have options again.

Nam-myoho-renge-kyo and the teaching of Nichiren Buddhism have given me back my life. It permeated my being to soothe and release the pain that had worked itself deep into my life. I felt the result even before I could understand what was happening.

Nothing but pain can come from violence and war. In the long run, there are never any winners—only losers. Buddhism seeks to embrace and understand our differences. It teaches us about the commonality among all people. It challenges us to create peace within our own hearts so that we can finally offer an alternative to violence.

I know that there will be people coming back from Iraq with the same pain that I carried. I can see it in the faces of some I meet, even before they say a word to me. They don't have to become another statistic, another casualty of war. There is an alternative and I have something to offer them. I have peace.

career and success

Unless we live fully right now, not sometime in the future, true fulfillment in life will forever elude us. Rather than putting things off till the future, we should find meaning in life, thinking and doing what is most important right now, right where we are—setting our hearts aflame and igniting our lives.

—Daisaku Ikeda

Absolute happiness can be constructed any time. In fact, the best time for its construction is in the midst of the struggle to achieve some goal. Goals are the means for the construction of inner happiness, not the necessary prerequisite for experiencing relative happiness.

When the inner aspects of life begin to change as a result of a diligent Buddhist practice, external circumstances begin to mirror those changes. Self-esteem moves in accordance with the thought that we are a Buddha—the one who has become awakened to the ultimate truth of life. False opinions and concepts of one's self begin to fade as the bigger picture takes precedence. Suddenly, a child from an abusive home realizes they deserve love, a person born in poverty discovers their worth, opportunity is born out of new beliefs based on truth. Frequently, the passion of a dream becomes the driving force for those internal changes.

Setting goals and establishing challenges inspire us to change our lives. In practicing Nichiren Buddhism, our desires become the catalysts for internal change, which subsequently changes our external environment until suddenly a goal is realized and a challenge is faced as the landscape of our lives change. One step at a time and our successes, or our failures, which spur more desire for success, build upon one another until a dream job is won, or a seemingly impossible career has manifested. We call ourselves successful in terms of the world's standards, but in fact, because of our Buddhist practice and study, spurred by our desires, we have awakened to the ultimate truth of life.

Breaking Through

Irene Wilson

*When your determination changes, everything will begin
to move in the direction you desire. The moment you
resolve to be victorious, every nerve and fiber in your
being will immediately orient itself toward your success.
On the other hand, if you think, "This is never going to
work out," then at that instant every cell in your being
will be deflated and give up the fight. Then everything
will move in the direction of failure.*

—Daisaku Ikeda

BEING AN UNEDUCATED WOMAN in America presented many barriers and limitations for me. It was at
that time that my hope, happiness or thoughts of a bright
future were at their lowest. I had no goals, no sense of
direction, no hopes, no dreams. I existed from one paycheck to the next. I knew that work meant survival, and
that's all I was doing—surviving. I spent too much money
on drinking—one month the electricity was turned off,
another month the water. When I began attending Nichiren
Buddhist meetings, it was like a light went on in my life.

Buddhism gave me options and solutions to life's problems. With these solutions came a feeling from deep inside
me—motivation. I wanted to do better and become a better
person. It was at these Buddhist activities that I began to
feel limited due to my lack of education.

I had quit school at fourteen, and suddenly I became hungry to study and understand Buddhism. However, reading the *World Tribune* (the SGI-USA's weekly newspaper) was not easy! I continued to chant. I struggled to recite the prayers. The motivation to develop my life began to grow stronger. I decided to go back to school and earn my GED as an adult.

I somehow passed the exam even though I still struggled with reading. Also, studying the material in Buddhism showed me my reading limitations. That was it; I made up my mind to get tutoring from the Wichita Adult Literacy Council. It was hard for me to take that first step. I had to work up my courage, and it had to come from me; no one else could do this for me.

Chanting gave me the courage to break through my limitations and overcome my fears. It became a constant effort that I would have to continue if I were to come out victorious.

I felt like SGI President Ikeda was talking especially to me when he once said, "Intellect will play a very important role in the coming age. By intellect I mean refined wisdom, clear reasoning, profound philosophy and broad-ranging knowledge. We are entering an age when people will develop intelligence and wisdom, infusing society with their new outlooks." I was inspired by these words. I encouraged others who were illiterate to get an education and to better their lives. I'd tell them, "If I can do it, so can you!"

Just four years after I began my tutoring, I was asked to become a member of the Wichita Falls Adult Literacy Council Board. In addition to taking part in regular monthly meetings and committee meetings, I volunteered to speak on the radio and television about overcoming illiteracy.

Enrollment at the Council increased, and the coordinator said that I was an inspiration to others, that I motivated them because I showed no fear in talking about my own challenge with illiteracy. The board members told me that I have leadership qualities; I know that comes from my Buddhist practice.

I have come a long way from the woman who lived day-to-day, from the woman with no hopes or dreams, to someone who can now motivate others to better themselves.

I've made big changes since gaining more self-confidence. One such change was being able to go before the local city government and petition for lights to be installed on our dark street. Then one night when I turned onto my street, it was lit up like a Christmas tree! I made a difference, not only for myself, but for my neighbors. It felt great. The other big change is that I now own a home on that brightly lit street.

I have won awards for speaking out for the Literacy Council and for volunteering for the United Way. I was nominated for the Helen Farabee Volunteer's Award, which is usually bestowed upon people who have PhDs! I received the first Jefferson Award presented in Wichita Falls and I won a scholarship to attend a leadership training program. By volunteering in our community, I was able to show proof that a person can overcome seemingly insurmountable obstacles.

Without my Buddhist practice, I'm not sure where I would have ended up. I probably wouldn't have lived to see my senior years. For one thing, I was headed toward disaster and for another, I was terrified of aging. It meant nothing but suffering, pain and relying on other people for your existence, a destitute existence.

But today, because of my Buddhist practice and the joyful life I've created, I have a wonderful life and I'm nearing my seventies. I have a beautiful family, including a great-grandson. After thirty-four years of working, I retired from Midwestern State University. I still have a full life continuing my education and volunteer work, raising a garden and fishing. Most of all I will continue my Buddhist activities to help others.

It was because of Nichiren Buddhism that I was able to change the course and direction of my life. Now well into my senior years, every nerve and fiber of my being is brimming with appreciation. I'm not afraid of getting older and I'm not afraid of death. I have known success and overcoming challenges in my life. Why should aging and death be any different? After all, I still practice Nichiren Buddhism.

BEAUTY, BENEFIT AND GOOD
ROBERT M. HASEGAWA

Before directing the lightning in the sky, we must first harness the storms in our own hearts.
—ROBERTO BRENES MESÉN

I WAS BORN IN A concentration camp for American citizens of Japanese ancestry near Minidoka, Idaho, during World War II. My family was given only a few days to pack what they could carry. They were shipped to a desolate barbed wire enclosure complete with guard towers. We lost the family farm, along with the tractors and trucks. Even our crops in the field were stolen. Our family of six lived in one small room in a wooden shack.

After the war, I grew up mostly on the South Side of Chicago, where my parents worked hard to raise four boys. My mother worked as a nurse at the University of Chicago and my father was a cook and later a chef at a country club. My parents would invite young medical doctors and PhDs for dinner in order to inculcate the value of college and learning into us boys.

I left home to work at the Seattle World's Fair and then returned to Chicago to attend the University of Illinois—Urbana. My main intention there was to get a law degree, but I also knew that by being in college I could postpone being drafted for the Vietnam War.

Inevitably, I was drafted, but as it turned out, I flunked

my physical. With only a few months of school left, I fell into a deep funk over being broke, in debt with no real job lined up and with the war and murders of Dr. Martin Luther King Jr. and Robert Kennedy raging in the background of my life. I was afraid to take the bar exam because the pass rate was only 40 percent. And to top it all off, my one true love had left me. She went off to attend grad school at New York University. So I just stayed in bed most of the day and night.

One morning, I had a feeling that I would meet someone who would change my life. I went to the student union where, after eight hours, I encountered a happy but weirdly diverse group of white, black and Asian people who introduced me to Nichiren Buddhism. I began chanting, received the Gohonzon and moved into a house with other students, where we held many Buddhist discussion meetings each week.

Conspicuous benefits, as we call them in Buddhism— obvious positive changes in one's life—appear all throughout one's Buddhist practice but especially when a person first begins chanting. Such was the case for me. My former landlady told me to forget about the three months back rent I owed her; a friend told me about the emergency interest-free loan money the law school had for poor students like me; and a nice lady came to town and gave me a job as a Federal Civil Rights Investigator—clearly, conspicuous benefits!

Although I chanted to pass the bar exam, I did not study for it. Three days before the exam, Carlos, my housemate, asked me why I wasn't studying. "I'm chanting about it," I said. Rolling his eyes, he explained that I had to chant *and* study harder than anyone else. Buddhism is about mastering cause and effect, *not* defying it. Now he tells me!

So I chanted and studied twenty hours a day for the next three days. Often I crammed while I was chanting, but I passed. My parents were so happy about it that they began chanting themselves.

Inconspicuous benefits in Buddhism are profound changes in one's life that may appear unnoticed over a longer period of time. They are changes in character, attitudes and one's negative beliefs that are often responsible for attracting unfavorable circumstances.

After working for the government for a year, I had a series of high-paying but stressful lawyer jobs. After a few years in each, I became bored and burned out. While I made lots of money, I managed to spend most of it. But I did continue to chant every day, open my home for meetings and talk to many people about Buddhism. Doing these things was personally gratifying and spiritually nurturing. Now I wanted to find work that would be as fulfilling.

I never liked Chicago all that much and after chanting about what I wanted out of life, researching and talking to people, I decided to move to Las Vegas.

Living conservatively, I didn't have to work for a couple of years. But after a month I became bored. The manager of my apartment-hotel asked me to work there since I always seemed to be hanging around. I agreed. Later, when the manager stole all of the hotel's money and gambled it away, the hotel owners asked me to become manager. I said, "OK." But I found myself working long hours, six days a week, on stuff I found meaningless.

It was time for another focused session of chanting in order to be totally honest with myself about what I wanted. I realized that I had been happiest working as a federal investigator on housing discrimination cases. I discovered that my recurring propensity was to work too many of my waking hours, with very little personal satisfaction. I had become a mediocre employee, with a cynical attitude and lackadaisical work habits.

Tsunesaburo Makiguchi, the first president of our Buddhist organization, taught that there are three kinds of value: beauty, benefit and good. In the working world, the value of beauty means to find a job you like; the value of benefit is to get a job that earns a salary that can support your daily life; the value of good means to find a job that helps others and contributes to society.

When I determined to learn these values, and to become someone's best employee, I was selected from among one hundred and twenty-five applicants to be an investigative auditor with the city of Las Vegas. I chanted sincerely for each person I worked with for the next twenty years. As a result, I enjoyed friendly cooperative relationships throughout my career. Gradually, I began to out-produce the rest of the audit division combined and was promoted. Having regular hours and free time, I taught aviation law to Air Force personnel and volunteered as coordinator for the Governor's Teen Suicide Prevention Program.

On a whim, I applied for the city's transportation manager's job. Once again, I was hired over one hundred and seventy-five applicants. When I got in there, I found out the transit terminal and trolley system had been "losing" more than a million dollars a year for eight years. If the bleeding did not stop, the drivers and maintenance workers would lose their jobs. I saw fear in their eyes. I was not concerned for myself. I had a permanent civil service rank, but I knew I had to do something for them.

According to SGI President Ikeda, dialogue helps solve any problem; and so we talked. I talked with hundreds of people: employees, customers and business owners. They talked to one another. As a result, we changed the transit routes in order to take our customers—more than ten thousand low-income seniors—to within twenty feet of the front doors of supermarkets, discount stores and medical clinics. Our innovation became a national model. An eighty-year-old woman came up to me and thanked me. She told me that she could now afford both food and her medication, since she did not have to use taxicabs for shopping.

Through legal research, I discovered that the Regional Commission owed the city 50 percent of our annual operating budget. After talking to the mayor, she demanded the money for us and got it!

A crony of an ex-councilman operated the roach-infested transit terminal snack bar. McDonald's won the competitive bid that I published. Additionally, by negotiating contracts for pay phones, vending machines, slot gaming operations and bus stop shelters, my division turned a *profit*. And, the city's former nemesis, the Regional Commission, gave us $1.8 million for new buses.

In addition to my regular duties, I was given the job of negotiating the public-private partnerships for the entire city. I produced about forty million dollars in combined new revenue and savings. As a "reward," I was promoted to acting assistant city manager during the incumbent's maternity leave.

I retired comfortably at age fifty-six having had the most fulfilling career thanks to following my heart and the direction I received as a result of my Buddhist practice. I have left the places where I have worked better off for having been there, and I have touched people's lives. That would never have happened if I had held on to my cynical attitude, which was only giving me mediocre jobs.

Oh, and remember the girl I was depressed over losing? She became my wife.

BUDDHISM AND THE LAW

MATT MACMILLAN

Courage comes from the wish to do what's right,
to build a just society and to be a good human being.
—DAISAKU IKEDA

SINCE I WAS A CHILD, I have wanted to be a police officer. I suppose that came out of watching entirely too much *Batman* and *The Lone Ranger* on television. Those two heroes were always there to ensure that everyone answered to justice, and this meant a lot to me as a small, awkward child. It would not be until decades later that I would understand how concepts like "justice" and "cause and effect" would connect the worlds of federal law enforcement and Buddhism for me.

I began chanting Nam-myoho-renge-kyo while I was in the Army. It was at about the same time that my mother, a post office clerk, sent me a recruitment flyer about postal inspectors. I learned that they have investigative jurisdiction in all criminal matters involving the integrity and security of the US Postal Service. The position requires the ability to communicate with people from all walks of life, proficiency with firearms, skills in self-defense and the ability to exercise good judgment. I felt like I could make a difference in this field. It would satisfy my superhero need while using two very important values that I have developed as a result of practicing Nichiren Buddhism, compassion and dialogue.

I completed my college education, graduated from the inspector academy and was assigned to Sacramento—in an eight-person field office. My first partner, Jim, served as a great mentor and showed me the ropes.

It was a mix of my professional training, my personal beliefs and practice of Buddhism, and the tenacity that I learned from Jim that helped me in one particular mail theft case. I was called out to investigate the loss of a registered mailing containing more than four thousand dollars in cash. I knew there were three employees who had access to the mailing. During my drive to the post office, I chanted to resolve the case quickly.

When I arrived, I put aside all judgments of guilt and began a dialogue with these three people. I talked a little, explained the consequences, appealed to their common sense and ethics and then I listened.

I earned my salary that night when one of the employees finally took me to his house and gave me back the stolen money. Even though he would have to face federal charges, he shook my hand that night and thanked me. I never raised my voice to him, cursed at him, chastised him or judged him. I think a lot of it had to do with allowing him to feel safe enough to tell me what happened and knowing that I would treat him with fairness.

Exercising good judgment is the cornerstone of law enforcement and practicing Nichiren Buddhism. SGI President Ikeda writes: "Buddhism is reason. It doesn't exist apart from society, apart from reality. That is why it is important for each of us to cultivate good judgment and common sense. We must respect and harmonize with society's ways. Respecting the life of each individual, we work among the people. This is the SGI's fundamental creed."

I was soon going to get a chance to test my own reason. I responded to a post office in downtown Sacramento where someone had deliberately punctured the gas tank of a mail truck. The suspect was a postal employee who had been on stress leave and was known to be extremely angry with postal management. He had been on the "workplace violence" radar for a long time. Within hours of the initial call, I was parked at his apartment complex, waiting for any signs of movement. This man did not have a criminal history, but he had a dozen firearms registered in his name and was known to be a paramilitary enthusiast. I waited for my supervisor to join me, and ten minutes after he arrived, our suspect walked out of his apartment toward his van and into our hands for questioning.

Back at the office, I learned that he had not eaten a meal in two days, his pay had been suspended, and he was being evicted from his apartment; he was unable to make contact with his estranged wife and children, and he was contemplating the murder of postal employees and himself. While we talked, I ordered a pizza for him.

After he confessed, he told us a story that sent a shiver down my spine. He said that if anyone had knocked at his door—his landlord, the police, his neighbors, anyone—he would have shot to kill. He was deadly serious, and we found an illegal automatic assault rifle with a fifty-round drum of ammunition propped next to his front door.

I am very glad that I did not go to his door by myself to try to talk with him on his turf because he was mentally and physically prepared to kill someone. My consistent daily Buddhist practice has helped me listen to my intuition, and I believe that through my morning prayers, which include a prayer for protection by the forces inherent in nature, I had been protected.

So what does it take to be a Buddhist postal inspector? It means to use good judgment and rely upon safe practices. Inasmuch as we can evoke the protective functions in our surroundings as we practice Buddhism, there is no room in law enforcement, or in a Buddhist practice, to neglect common sense or fundamental training. On the job, I don't take unnecessary risks. Above all I always try to treat people with dignity and respect. I chant for the highest good of all concerned, in any situation.

I suspect, all these years later, that it was Batman and the Lone Ranger's sense of integrity and fair play that I admired in their attempts to serve justice. Being a Buddhist integrates all those elements for me, and I bring those elements into the world of federal law enforcement. It is the most honorable way I know to practice law, short of being a superhero.

SELLING MYSELF ON ME

JOHN HAYDON

Try not to become a man of success, but rather try to become a man of value.

—ALBERT EINSTEIN

I'D BEEN IN SALES for twelve years and have always viewed myself as a C-plus, or average, producer. The second half of 2004 I had acquired the highest number of new clients of any sales representative in my company. The deals I closed were small, however, and my overall results were still C-plus.

Throughout my career, I wondered: *What is it about A performers? Is it good fortune? Luck? Ability?* Whatever it was, I believed I didn't have it and wouldn't—at least not in this lifetime. There were a couple of sales reps at my company who were continuously high performers. I often cringed with jealousy, trying to hide my self-hatred whenever they closed a big sale.

I loved the company I worked for, and I worked hard; harder, in fact, than most of the other reps. But it was not enough.

From January to June 2005, I had reached only 33 percent of my sales quota. I was in a slump, and my confidence was taking a huge beating. As the high performers continued to bring in big deals, I felt increasingly lost. I didn't know what to do. I felt like I was drowning.

On June 30, I was called into the vice president's office. He asked me to sign a Performance Improvement Plan that went something like this:

- Achieve a certain sales result each month for the next three months (July through September) or be fired. This number was a stretch for even the best reps.
- Work a minimum of nine hours a day.
- Take no vacation time during this period (which meant my family had to cancel a cottage rental on Cape Cod).

The 20 percent salary increase that all reps received on July 1 would be withheld until my sales goals were met.

I left work that day deeply discouraged. I was about to lose my job, and I was letting my family down. Most of all, I felt discouraged in my Buddhist practice. *Why is this happening?* I thought in frustration. *I've been chanting for many years. Surely I deserve more than this.*

I moped around for a couple of days and then realized that complaining about my situation and getting down on myself would not get me the result I needed. I was up against a wall and absolutely had to achieve these requirements—there was no Plan B. Obviously, I could always get another job, but I would bring the experience of defeat to that job. I had to change something very deep. On July 1, I decided I was going to put my spiritual muscle behind this goal. I chanted several hours a day to change the deep-seated thoughts that kept attracting the results I was experiencing: thoughts stemming from my upbringing, from my past and deeper still, from my karma.

As I chanted, I remembered something a fellow Buddhist had said to me, "Even people who have been chanting for many years cannot change deep karma if they think it is an immutable part of their true identity." I realized that, yes, the self-identity I had created as a salesperson was one of limitation. I had a self-limiting belief that said I'm only a C-plus salesperson; that although I'm a nice guy and very earnest at work, I will never be a top performer. *Maybe sales isn't what I'm supposed to be doing,* I would tell myself.

Now, I was up against the wall. I had no choice but to change something seemingly impossible—a deeply held belief about myself. For the first time, I knew in my gut that I would win. Chanting several hours a day has to produce a result, especially now that I had a clear sense of mission.

In July, I closed only one new deal and hit only half of that month's goal. I continued to chant, realizing that my efforts would take time to bring results. I refused to be swayed.

In August, I closed five new deals and achieved almost twice that month's goal. I was on my way but not yet close to declaring victory.

In September, a very strange thing happened. On the morning of September 12, with no deals closed for the month and only fourteen days left to keep my job, I herniated a disc. I was at the gym when I felt something very painful in my lower back. I ended up at home in bed, in tears and unable to move. I was taken by ambulance to the hospital where, in addition to the injury, the doctors found bone masses in my lower back that were possibly cancerous.

During the next week in the hospital I underwent every kind of test. My wife and friends came to visit and chant with me, and when I was alone, I would find comfort in chanting. The doctors found it strange that all my blood tests were negative for cancer or other illnesses.

I went back to work part time the following week with only nine days left and no sales. Then, during the last week of the quarter, it all came together. Clients I had been expecting to make sales to in December wanted to buy now. Another company called and wanted to buy from me because the competition wasn't treating them well. This one deal alone made up about 75 percent of my quota. In the end, I closed five deals and hit three times that month's goal.

For the entire quarter, I achieved more than twice the sales numbers laid out in my Performance Improvement Plan, I was the top sales rep and received the salary increase that previously had been withheld. I also took three vacation days in October with my family,

I recall SGI President Ikeda once saying that the determination to win is the better part of winning. This experience was not about getting results on my job but about challenging my self-limiting beliefs.

BELIEVING IN MYSELF

ROBERT M. REEL

*Who answers our prayers? We do—through faith
and effort. No one does it for us.*
—DAISAKU IKEDA

YOU CAN MASH 'EM, fry 'em, boil 'em or bake 'em;
add salt and pepper, or butter and sour cream; or
maybe just cheese. I'm talking about a few ways you can
eat potatoes. I can vividly recall what it was like, on a very
limited income, to eat potatoes. Just potatoes!

I didn't have an auspicious beginning. As a high school
senior in El Paso, Texas, I led a dangerous life of excessive
partying. That, combined with poor family interaction and
ordinary teenage troubles, added up to a rebellious kid with
no direction. I was lost, but I was searching for something
deeper and more meaningful. One night I went to a
Nichiren Buddhist meeting with a group of friends. I sensed
that it was "right," that chanting Nam-myoho-renge-kyo
was what I needed, what I craved.

I changed jobs continually, lacking any real sense of hope
of finding a fulfilling job, or career for that matter. I struggled
just to eat. I cannot recall the number of times my utilities
were turned off, the number of miles I have hitchhiked or all
of the places I lived. Fortunately, several families practicing
Buddhism looked after me.

Fueled and guided by the example that SGI President

Ikeda consistently set, I studied his writings daily. I progressively understood that Buddhism was a deep, sacred philosophy that I could apply to my life and my misconception of who I was. Slowly but surely, I faced my low self-esteem, limited respect for authority and more. Because of President Ikeda's example and that of many members—how they practiced Buddhism and applied the principles to their lives to find happiness—I began to evolve into a person I liked, a person who had more inner peace, someone who could actually get things done.

As a result, I was finally able to support myself. I landed a job as an equipment orderly in a hospital. My job was to clean respiratory therapy equipment and supplies. I actually kept a job! I wanted to really succeed. Within a year, I was offered the opportunity for more on-the-job training in minor clinical support procedures. I became interested in respiratory care—helping to diagnose and treat cardiac and pulmonary diseases. The hospital allowed me a flexible schedule while I attended community college, and they even paid for my tuition—100 percent of it! I graduated with an associate degree and successfully completed my registry examinations.

After a couple of years as a respiratory therapist and never letting up on my Buddhist practice, or participating in Buddhist activities, I became an assistant manager for a small local respiratory care department. Within a few months, I was promoted to a director and relocated to a slightly larger cardio-pulmonary department in the small town of Nacogdoches, Texas.

I continued to develop by challenging myself to achieve many personal, career and spiritual objectives. I was facing increasing challenges as a manager in healthcare with only an associate degree but it would always be my Buddhist practice that helped me through. It enabled me to somehow renew myself and address the immediate issues at hand.

Again, I relocated to a larger cardio-pulmonary department. This time it was in Farmington, New Mexico. Shortly after that, a job with a multi-hospital system in Albuquerque became available. Even though this potentially new position was about five times larger than my current one, I decided to go for it, and I got it.

The new job, another relocation and wanting to take on more responsibilities in my Buddhist community, forced me to address my fears of not being good enough. I studied Buddhist principles about the dignity of who we are, and I chanted to imbue my life with that truth, instead of continuing to run old false beliefs in my head. With my daily practice of chanting and studying, I began to be encouraged to expand my hope, wisdom and courage, to succeed regardless of my fears. Quite unexpectedly, the hospital system asked me to assume a larger administrative role—responsibility for surgical services for three hospitals.

At one point, the entire healthcare industry, including my hospital system, transitioned through a stressful period of downsizing and restructuring. Without my Buddhist practice, I'm sure I would have been overwhelmed by these circumstances and again become self-destructive, as was my pattern when I was younger. Instead, my responsibilities at work doubled.

I recognized that furthering my education would allow me to contribute even more to my work, so I eventually decided to go back to school. I worked and attended classes full time. Time itself was a rare commodity, but school was great! I had prepared myself for a struggle, but I did not expect to love it as much as I did.

I earned my bachelor's degree in public administration. I felt so strong and joyful because of my accomplishment that I only took one semester off before beginning a master's program in business. The hospital system, once again, paid for my tuition, for both degrees! For someone who had no means of even earning a living when I began practicing Buddhism, having the cost of three degrees paid for by my employers was amazing, and a true testament to me. I've also been able to express my gratitude by making significant contributions back to my previous employer's foundations, which earmark funds for staff education.

Last summer, I was recruited by one of the largest not-for-profit healthcare systems in the country. The recruiter enticed me to consider applying for a key administrative role in their Sacramento region. California had never even occurred to me. But I applied for the position and got it.

Now in California, I'm in awe of the trajectory of my life. I work as a vice president in the system's Sacramento operations, responsible for all specialty services. My external world had no choice but to change considering how I was continuing to expand the respect and love I have for myself thanks to my Buddhist practice. It's a new world for me as I now dig deeper into my life to find the strength necessary to contribute to my new employer and to create value in my community and in my world.

It's been, and continues to be, a journey I love. And through it all, I still like potatoes.

The Turning Point

Erica Shelton

This lifetime will never come again; it is precious
and irreplaceable. To live without regret,
it is crucial for us to have a concrete purpose
and continually set goals and challenges.
—Daisaku Ikeda

IN DECEMBER 2002, I boarded a plane like any other passenger at the Los Angeles International Airport. But unlike most people going home for the holidays, I wasn't eager to reach my destination. A few days earlier, I had sunk into a deep depression. My despair had become so severe that suicide seemed like the only solution.

What brought me to this dark place was a series of personal failures. Earlier that year, I had made strides toward a career in television writing—a goal I had been pursuing for years. I had landed a reputable agent who, a few months later, dropped me as a client. It was disappointing, but at least I had a flourishing new relationship with a man who, I confessed to a friend, I believed was "the one"—the man I would marry. Then, in November, he returned from a business trip to tell me he wanted to pursue a relationship with a woman he had met during his travels.

After these devastating setbacks, I was convinced that not only did bad things happen but that they would most certainly happen to me.

This was a lesson I carried over from childhood. I was three when my mother left my father and me. Being reared by a single father was difficult enough, but my situation was compounded by frequent moves and the constant presence of drugs. My mother maintained a presence, although my resentment regarding her decision to leave tainted our relationship.

Through all the hardship there was one constant element in my life—writing. It provided solace against the turbulent, ever-changing landscape of my childhood, especially during my angst-ridden pre-teen years. During this period, my father's drug abuse worsened. He was absent for long stretches, and the instability of my home life took its toll.

In junior high, the sadness that plagued me worsened. On a Friday in February, I attempted to end my life. Although I did not succeed, the darkness that led to this act lingered. I was sent to a facility for troubled girls. Straightjackets and solitary confinement were the order, and a plastic fork and private showers were privileges few received.

After several months of therapy, I returned to school but continued to feel lost and overwhelmed. Kind words from teachers—like Mrs. Lasky, who returned a story I had written for seventh-grade English with the simple words, "You should do this, in life I mean"—helped me through.

Because teachers took note of my interests and talents, I started working toward college and a career in television writing, which gave me a sense of direction and focus. I earned a scholarship to Northwestern University, and after college, I worked at a Chicago television station. Later, I received a prestigious scholarship to the graduate screen-writing program at the University of Southern California in Los Angeles.

By winter, however, I was back where I started—depressed, feeling like a failure and contemplating suicide. I had a love-hate relationship with words. There were the words I wrote and then the words I said to myself. Years of self-destructive thoughts barred me from pursuing my dreams. On some level, I had decided long ago that things were not going to work out for me.

By the time I boarded the plane to Detroit in December 2002, I knew I couldn't go on this way. I wanted to transform my life, but I had no idea how to do it.

I tried psychological counseling. I admitted that I was lacking a spiritual connection and was seeking a sense of empowerment. During one session, I mentioned that I was curious about Buddhism.

A short time later, I was sitting in a hair salon talking about Mother's Day with a new hairdresser when she mentioned her Buddhist practice. In the quiet of the nearly empty salon, she introduced me to Nichiren Buddhism.

I began to chant and almost immediately things started to change. We screenwriters call this the turning point. And it was. I signed with a literary manager and also with a major talent agency, far better than my former agent who was no longer returning my calls.

But the old feeling of self-doubt resurfaced. Each time I sat down to write, I felt paralyzed. Chanting didn't appear to be improving the situation. In fact, it got worse.

I was scheduled to officially join the SGI-USA, but felt I couldn't possibly go through with it. I obviously wasn't ready. I attempted to postpone it, but I lost my nerve. Later, while driving, I pulled over and sobbed. A script I was supposed to give my agent was long overdue, and I felt like a failure. I began chanting right there in my car.

It was in this dark hour that I realized that I needed to let go of fearing the outcome. I couldn't complete my writing project because I was so fearful that, like a number of things in my childhood, this dream wasn't going to work out. Even though it went against everything I had known and lived, I had to surrender to the fact that, no matter what happened, even if I wrote the worst script in the history of the world, I would reach my goal. Things were going to work out. And they did.

I officially joined the SGI that night and set a goal to get hired on a show with good writers.

As I chanted each morning and evening, I felt butterflies in my stomach. After a few months of chanting, I noticed the butterflies were gone. The change was almost imperceptible, and I felt my faith deepening.

In March, my agent called. The creator of *CSI: Crime Scene Investigation*, wanted to meet me. Days later, he offered me a job on the new spin-off *CSI: New York*.

The morning I received the news I had read the following words from SGI President Ikeda: "The spirit of this day lies not in magnificent ceremonies or high-sounding words. It lies in being victorious . . . No matter what excuses we try to make, giving in to defeat brings misery and loses us the respect of others. I hope each of you without exception will adorn your life with indestructible triumph."

In December, the episode that I co-wrote was shot and aired in February. I have achieved this dream. My Buddhist practice, however, has given me far more than a job. I now have the tools and ability to overcome the darkness that gripped me since childhood. After years of suffering, I'm free to pursue my wildest dreams.

Dreaming Big

Waneta Boutin Tew

No pessimist ever discovered the secrets of the stars,
or sailed to an uncharted land, or opened a
new doorway for the human spirit.
—Helen Keller

I MUST SAY, becoming a Nichiren Buddhist is one of the highlights of my life. I started chanting some five months before I actually joined the SGI. I was a "closet chanter" who did not want anyone to know.

I was born legally blind. When I was four years old I had surgery on my eyes, but before they could heal, I was kicked in the head and my left eye hemorrhaged. The damage was done. I lost all vision, even light perception, in my left eye. My right eye had degenerative myopia and a dislocated lens, which meant I only saw out of half of the lens.

My parents sent me to a school for the blind in Massachusetts until I was eighteen. My last three years of schooling, I went to public school. After graduating, I took a job in Montpelier, Vermont, running a cafeteria. Because I was the first person in that position to ever turn a profit, I was advised to get further training in whatever area interested me.

I decided to go to Arkansas where they have a program for the blind, where I could get advanced training. Little did I know that, at the same time, my husband-to-be, Danny,

121

was leaving Greensboro, North Carolina, to attend the same program. Usually many clients arrived each day, but that day it was just the two of us.

Our friendship, which later blossomed into love, began from that first day. Danny taught me about Nichiren Buddhism and about chanting Nam-myoho-renge-kyo. We were married on Christmas Eve of that year.

After we finished our courses, I moved to Greensboro with Danny. At the time I did not drive and never dreamed that I could. Danny didn't have a license either, obviously, because he was blind, too.

I began to talk to a Buddhist friend about my vision, and I decided to chant for my eyesight to improve. I wanted something seemingly impossible: I wanted to be able to drive. My friend told me to chant to find the right eye doctor who would understand my condition. He also told me that I should also chant to get a car and a driver's license.

I began chanting two hours a day and saw the changes that began to occur in my life and in Danny's life. I finally decided to tell Danny and his mother what I wanted, and what I had talked about with my friend. I told them that I was determined to have a car and to be able to drive it within a year.

Danny and his mother were skeptical, but I was focused on achieving this goal. My husband and I were on disability and certainly didn't have the money for a car, but that didn't stop me from pursuing my dream.

After years of being told that I would be totally blind, I found an eye doctor who thought he could help me. He completely understood what my eye condition was all about. I had found the right eye doctor! Exactly what I had been chanting for.

Soon, with his help, my eyesight improved enough for me to drive! Believe me, it was a challenge. I did not know the brake from the gas pedal, but Danny's mother taught me. She has not only been a wonderful support in our lives, but she has also been there to help us financially. In February, we bought our first car!

Every year, in order to continue driving, I have to go to my eye doctor to get a form filled out for the Department of Motor Vehicles. In the early days of my practice, my vision was 20/80, now it runs between 20/60 and 20/70; it all depends on my prayers. When I'm not practicing Buddhism daily, my belief in myself and what I deserve tends to suffer along with my vision. My Buddhist practice reinforces my true worth and my eyes have no choice but to respond positively. Everything in my life responds more positively. Needless to say, I'm not a "closet chanter" anymore.

Success, Right Where You Are
Kat Paterno

*I must admit that I personally measure success
in terms of the contributions an individual makes
to her or his fellow human beings.*
—Margaret Mead

I WAS THE MOST UNLIKELY candidate for law school. I had gone to film school and made edgy documentaries, played bass guitar in punk bands and lived a very alternative lifestyle. I certainly never thought I would join the ranks of what I then thought were evil corporate American sellouts.

Over time, I slowly climbed my way out of the underground world and ended up managing restaurants and nightclubs. I eventually found myself living in Los Angeles, making less than thirty thousand dollars a year managing a live theater.

As much as I liked the people I worked with, I hated how lost and unfulfilling my career path looked. I decided to change directions and go back to school. I was twenty-nine years old, and I was plagued with a "save the world" complex that wasn't dissolving with my youth as I had been told by many it would. I had spent years pondering the perfect career—one that would sufficiently satisfy my passion to help humanity. After years of consideration, I realized that education was the key to creating a better world.

124

What I really wanted to do was to become a teacher, eventually move into educational reform and develop a curriculum that would enable children to become great human beings. But my parents talked me out of it. My mom is a teacher and has experience living on a teacher's salary. She was concerned that, as I was the least thrifty of her children, I might not be able to survive on a teacher's pay. I was easily persuaded at that time in my life because I was at a complete loss as to how people make money. Somehow I decided that law school would give me the power to effect change and give me more earning possibilities, and for some reason, I knew in my gut that it would give me a foundation for my dreams of educational reform.

Two months later, I was introduced to Nichiren Buddhism. By the time I started law school one year later, I was practicing daily and attending meetings weekly.

As a result of my Buddhist practice, I was admitted to a great law school—the University of California–Los Angeles—and was asked to join UCLA's prestigious law review. I was very interested in charter schools because they provide an arena for reforming education, so I wrote my law review article on charter school legislation.

While I did not enjoy law school, I did well and eventually landed a job at a large, international law firm. I passed the bar exam the first time I took it and started practicing law.

Tsunesaburo Makiguchi, the first president of the Soka Gakkai, taught that there are three kinds of value: beauty, benefit and good. Josei Toda, a teacher himself, and

Daisaku Ikeda, the subsequent Soka Gakkai presidents, have interpreted the meaning of Makiguchi's three kinds of value in terms of a career. President Toda said, "Everyone's ideal is to get a job they like (beauty) that offers financial security (benefit) and where they can contribute to society (good)."

When I first heard this, I was already a lawyer. I immediately thought two things. First, I had never had a single one of the three values satisfied in any job, prior to being a lawyer. And second, I realized that I had now accomplished one of the three: for the first time in my life, I was making lots of money. However, I wanted to have a job that I loved—a job that contributed to others and that was fulfilling. I wanted all three things referred to by President Makiguchi.

My job as a lawyer in a big firm became extremely stressful and demanding. I worked long hours, many times arriving home after midnight, and I often worked through the weekends. While I enjoyed some aspects of it, including the people I worked with, I was largely unhappy being a lawyer. I was often flooded with feelings of frustration, many times wanting to quit my job and go back to school to become a teacher. However, because of the large law school debt I had incurred, I was stuck. I was not yet financially able to switch to a career in education. Something had to change.

Education and helping people was still my dream, and I was not going to give it up. I started chanting to find a way to slowly begin to infuse education into my legal career. I thought about my firm's strong commitment to pro bono work (offering free legal services to worthy causes), and I suddenly had an idea. I talked to a partner at work about my interest in education, and I asked him if he would be willing to sponsor me in providing a charter school with free legal work. He said yes. Unfortunately, the charter school with which I had connections already had attorneys. I was so busy that I didn't have time to seek out another charter school.

In December, I started writing down my goals for the coming year. As I wrote down my determination to accomplish my dream of having a career that I loved, that paid really well and that was also fulfilling, I suddenly realized that I had a hard time believing I *deserved* all three of these things in one job. It seemed so far-fetched, and a part of me did not believe it was possible for me to be that happy in a career. This amazing epiphany led me to sit down and chant about why I thought I did not deserve to have the career of my dreams. As I chanted, I came to realize that by first helping myself, changing my life and achieving my goals and dreams, which included my dream of a career in education, I could more easily help others. I began to chant with the intention of helping others by helping myself and, by doing so, raise my self-worth to the point where deserving to be happy no longer was an issue.

Shortly after I began chanting this way, the partner who had originally agreed to sponsor the charter school called me into his office. Knowing of my heartfelt interest in education, he was excited to tell me that a charter school needed legal services in my exact line of specialty— labor and employment. I could not believe it. Not only was I able to work with a charter school, but also the specific case that I would take on was so important that it had the potential to affect charter schools and the teachers who work in them nationwide.

The executive director who ran the charter school was amazing. He had been a federal defense attorney, a law professor and a television writer. Six years earlier, he had invested hundreds of thousands of his own dollars and devoted all of his free time to starting a charter school premised on social justice and designed to teach underprivileged inner-city kids that they had the power to affect society. I worked with him for an entire month, and because he knew that I had a special interest in charter schools, he spent extra time teaching me everything he could about them. During one conversation, I told him of my dream to eventually segue into the education field. He said: "Who knows? Maybe someday you will take over for me as executive director of the school." It was the happiest I had been in my career so far.

I realized that without changing jobs, I had begun to manifest my dreams. I learned self-worth by extending my own worth and understanding that I deserved to be as happy as I wanted others to be. For the first time in my life, I know what it feels like to have accomplished all three aspects of a happy career: I am paid well, doing something that I love and helping others in ways that I have always dreamed about.

POLISHING MY LIFE

RICHARD STARKINGS

Command success with faith.

—JOSEI TODA

SINCE I WAS YOUNG, I always wanted to work in comic books. As a teenager, I developed an interest in lettering, a largely unregarded but essential art without which comics cannot be read. Pen lettering is an arduous task but I enjoyed the challenge and, after graduating from college, I picked up lettering work for various comic book publishers in London.

In a very short period of time, I was hired by Marvel Comics in London. I eventually rose to the position of editor of boys adventure comics when I was just twenty-five. I continued to letter comics on the side to earn extra money, but I loved editing comics: it paid well and London was a great place to spend my mid-twenties and money. I thought I was perfectly happy.

Unfortunately, no one at Marvel UK seemed capable of teaching other editors how to create good comic books. It was clear to me that enthusiasm and love of comics did not qualify me to help young writers learn *how* to tell good stories, any more than it enabled them to *produce* good stories.

When I was given the task of editing a comic based on the *Ghostbusters* cartoon series, I found myself having to

129

cast around for new writers in order to generate the large amount of material that was needed in the book. I bought scripts that were OK but they seemed to lack something, which I couldn't quite put my finger on. I wanted to read and publish stories that were both fun and meaningful.

A young artist I hired recommended the work of his old school friend, John, and brought him to meet me. Generally, I avoided hiring friends of friends but there was something about John that inspired me to give him a chance. John was quick with a joke and earnest in his desire to write entertaining stories. The scripts he turned in proved to be witty and vibrant and eagerly sought after by the artists working for me. I struggled in vain to understand what exactly it was that they contained so that I could communicate "the formula" to other writers.

I soon learned that John was a Nichiren Buddhist and after he and I had come to know each other, I asked him about his practice. I sat with him and his wife as they said their prayers and I leafed through one of his Buddhist books. I asked John if I could borrow the book.

Halfway through my reading I came across the phrase "turning poison into medicine." Suddenly, a penny dropped. All John's *Ghostbuster* stories turned negatives into positives. *The Ghostbusters* would be called to bust a ghost in a hotel but would persuade the ghost and the hotel manager to work together so that people would visit the hotel *because* it was haunted; or the *Ghostbusters* would trap two mischievous electrical sprites in a battery, thereby creating a source of everlasting power.

I called John the next day. "Gotcha!" I told him. "You're propagating Buddhism in your stories, aren't you?"

"Um, no, not deliberately," John said, "but I have been practicing for more than four years and I guess that Buddhist philosophy is starting to bubble up out of my life into my work."

I decided I wanted to get some Buddhist wisdom. I started chanting and encouraged other writers working for me to consider the concept of "turning poison into medicine" as an alternative to the "this ghost is toast" philosophy our licensor encouraged. Subsequently *The Real Ghostbusters* comic became one of Marvel UK's most successful publications.

My personal success at Marvel was short-lived. After embracing a Buddhist practice, I initiated a series of workshops to train editors in the basics of storytelling and comics production. Suddenly my editor in chief grew jealous and suspicious of my intent and accused me of making a power play. Stunned by her accusations, I wrote a letter of resignation. I had some money saved and decided I would use it to take a year off to travel.

My savings ran out in California. Friends in New York at the central offices of Marvel Comics gave me as much freelance lettering work as I could handle, so I continued to work for Marvel and DC Comics when I moved to Los Angeles.

Unfortunately, I now found myself struggling to enjoy the task of pen lettering. It had provided me with a way into comics but now seemed like a chore and a penance.

Even in sunny California the consequences of my deci-sion to quit my comfortable job at Marvel UK became more and more painful. I would often spend hours chant-ing simply for the strength to get through the day. I felt completely directionless, and lettering was agony.

At several Buddhist meetings, we talked about choices. For example, a dishwasher in a restaurant could choose to be totally unhappy with his lot in life. Or he could take it upon himself to make the plates and glasses shine so brightly that the customers would come back to that restaurant just because the place settings were so clean! I really took those words to heart. Generally, you don't pick up a comic book and rave about the lettering any more than you would sit in a restaurant and say: "Wow! These knives and forks are really shiny!" But neither can you properly appreciate a meal if your plate isn't clean.

In the depths of my misery I decided to be the best let-terer in the business!

The work that was sent to me from New York was always due the next day. Being the best letterer in the busi-ness seemed to be impossible with deadlines like that. I real-ized that making a living this way, while at the same time setting a high standard for myself, were almost mutually exclusive goals.

Then I bumped into a former Marvel editor who sug-gested that I digitize my lettering styles on a Macintosh computer. This seemed to me to offer a solution to the dilemma of quality versus quantity.

After a certain amount of trial and error, I produced a

workable digital version of my pen lettering style and convinced a couple of editors at Marvel to let me letter their books electronically. I hired an assistant and with him developed a number of fonts, which allowed us to become a tireless team of comic book letterers.

The quality of the digital work we were producing soon attracted offers of more work, and we were able to move out of the back of my apartment and into studios in Santa Monica. I hired another assistant, and another and another. At the peak of my success, I had sixteen employees on payroll and we won more than a dozen awards for our work.

Although we were still dependent on Marvel and DC comics for income, we slowly developed a secondary online business—publishing and selling the font software we developed for lettering. Now that secondary business offers more than two hundred fonts in its catalog and is supporting a third business, my own publishing imprint.

As an editor of comic books, my desire was to find a way to encourage writers to produce meaningful stories. That desire led me to Nichiren Buddhism, which led me to California and back to lettering comic books.

My desire to become the best lettering artist in the business precipitated a complete change, not only in the manner in which I worked but also in the entire comic book industry. The digital methods and processes we developed are now the global standard for lettering comics. Our fonts are used in comics, movies and advertising throughout the world. I even co-wrote and published a "How-To" book about our work.

In the course of my struggles, I acquired a work permit, a green card, created a family with my wife, Youshka, bought a house and started my own publishing imprint.

Along with greater success came a deep-seated, sure and certain knowledge that anything is possible. Shortly thereafter, I approached a top artist, with whom I had developed a close friendship, to bring to life my own comic book character, which I also determined to publish myself. The first issue was named by a mainstream British style magazine as one of the top ten hottest comic books of the year, and the second issue was nominated for two top industry awards. The story touches upon issues that range from ethnic cleansing, genetic engineering to racism. It also has a mutant hippo, time travel and a robotic frog. It is still a comic after all.

I overcame a multitude of problems and struggles along the way, but every time I got knocked down, I would get up, chant and polish those knives and forks again.

finances

Buddhist scriptures describe secular millionaires as being of a good family, possessing wealth, having dignity, being pure in their actions, exhibiting proper manners and enjoying great prestige. . . . It is worthwhile for us to strive to acquire the virtues of these millionaires. I hope that, basing yourselves on faith, you will become wealthy people of virtue and influence who are widely respected.

—Daisaku Ikeda

LIFE, LIBERTY AND the *purchase* of happiness have increasingly become the new American ideals. While it is undeniably enjoyable to purchase the "toys" we believe will make us happy, it is also true the joy we feel is not long lasting. The new-car excitement quickly fades amid the reality of continued car payments. New clothes wear out or go out of style. To recreate the joy of the initial purchase, we buy more and more, again and again.

Nichiren writes: "More valuable than treasures in a store-house are the treasures of the body, and the treasures of the heart are the most valuable of all. From the time you read this letter on, strive to accumulate the treasures of the heart!"

Treasures of the storehouse are material possessions and financial wealth. Treasures of the body are health, knowledge, status, etc. While these are important and neglecting them would cause us unnecessary suffering, they are all subject to the law of impermanence, and hence they are ultimately relative. They cannot be the foundation of lasting happiness.

Treasures of the heart are treasures of the inner realm, qualities and attributes arising from our Buddha nature. The real treasures of life are the qualities that enhance our actions in daily life, giving us the wisdom, courage, compassion and confidence to win over any circumstance. The foundation of human happiness begins in the inner realm. Happiness constructed here is not dependent, transient or circumstantial—it is resilient and, as Hamlet put it, resistant to the "slings and arrows of outrageous fortune."

The saying "money can't buy happiness" takes on a new twist when a profound spiritual practice such as Nichiren Buddhism is adopted. It is true that money may not bring you happiness, but happiness may very well bring you money as the following stories tell.

A Moment That Changed Time

Julie Larson

From what we get, we can make a living;
what we give, however, makes a life.
—Arthur Ashe

I HAD BEEN PRACTICING Nichiren Buddhism consistently for many years. My daughter, Joan, was six years old and I was raising her alone. I was sitting on the couch reading when Joan, standing at the window, said someone was taking our car.

Damn it, I thought. I hadn't made a car payment in almost three months. Still, I thought I had a couple of days left. I went to the window. There they were, towing my car to impound. A flood of names came to mind. People who might help me pay off all of the fees. I would tell them that the car company screwed up. They always gave me more than three months. I didn't want to bother you. Sorry. Please and sorry.

Suddenly, my daughter started to cry, hard. Her doll was in the car. I grabbed Joan and we ran outside to ask the guy for the doll—to say please, to say sorry.

By the time we got to the car it was all ready to go. Joan asked the man if she could please get her doll. I had her ask because who could say no to a crying little girl? Well, we found the one guy who could.

"Once the car is loaded everything in it is ours," he said

coldly. I spoke up on her behalf to no avail. The car and the doll left while my daughter stood there sobbing. We went back into the house. I was so beside myself with grief that Joan's wailing was just kind of a dull moan in the background. How would I get my car back? Once they were towed, it was not just a matter of the three months of payments. Add on top of that the towing and impound fees. It would be a thousand dollars, easy.

"Mommy, I won't be able to sleep without my doll," she said, when I finally got far enough out of my money-math haze to hear her.

"Sorry, Joan, I'll figure something out."

The worst thing about the situation was that I could have avoided the whole thing if I had been proactive, called the car company, saved the money, been on top of it. But I wasn't. And it wasn't the first time.

Feeling so totally defeated and absolutely wrong, I did what I always did—I chanted. This time though, it was different. I think I got to such a level of "wrongness" that I couldn't take it anymore. When I sat down to chant this time I became aware deep inside—maybe for the first time—that chanting works, regardless of your righteousness, or conversely, wrongness. It works whether you are wise or stupid, even if you are evil; all chanting leads to enlightenment. As I began, so sad and defeated, I felt no need to make an excuse for myself. I just sat and said the words *Nam-myoho-renge-kyo* over and over.

My first feeling was a relief of sorts. My tendency to tear at myself in these situations was beyond temptation. It was habit. This self-destruction would lead to depression, and depression makes it really hard to parent. That causes more guilt, which makes for bad parenting, and on and on until you're caught in a vicious web of self-hate.

Abandoning that route, at first I was just relieved. It was as if my altar, where the Gohonzon was enshrined, was an abused women's shelter where I could go and hide from myself. After about two minutes, I had a realization. If I could make a determination—a change in my thinking and in my heart that would profoundly change my life—in the midst of the worst of it, then everything from then on would have to be easier in comparison. Already, my desire to destroy myself had been quelled. Now it occurred to me that if in this crucial moment I could not only *not* destroy myself but invest in myself just by chanting with a new determination, I would never have to revisit this kind of mess. But I knew I had to do it from the bottom of my heart. I cannot explain how I knew this; I just did.

Then I began to remember snippets of writings from SGI President Ikeda that had been encouraging to me in the past, and now in light of my present circumstances, these words were sinking into a deeper place of understanding within me. One phrase was "From this moment, from myself, I will create history." I wrote that one down on a card and put it on my altar. It made me laugh that I could even be thinking about making history in this moment. But then again, maybe creating history was just making the simple adjustment where my daughter would see me rebound quickly. Where I would regain my balance and be there for her. Maybe that simple adjustment would help her grow up more healthy and whole, effecting a change that in ten generations would make a significant historic difference. And in fact, after an hour or so of this, I felt totally centered.

I heard my daughter in the other room, sad, sad, sad. I went to her, whole, intact and healed. I was able to encourage her quickly. Immediately, I could see the importance and the effect of chanting right away—the importance of not slandering myself in a moment when it seemed like the only thing to do. I was so happy and yet still, I had no idea how much my life had changed that day.

From that day on, I never revisited that kind of intense poverty. I was able to keep on top of things because I didn't become self-destructive every time I made a mistake or, worse, when I was out and out wrong. I had developed the ability to self-reflect and make a new determination quickly.

Since then, I wrote for *Dharma & Greg* for three years, and then three years for *The Drew Carey Show*. I also traveled around the world performing with Drew Carey and the rest of the *Whose Line is it Anyway?* I own my own home in Santa Monica, and while life might still be a struggle, I am able to self-reflect and take new and bold action with each issue that crops up. I have developed immense fortune and the ability to use it to create value.

"Earthly desires equal enlightenment" is a concept in Nichiren Buddhism. Other philosophies sometimes say that earthly desires are the "root of all evil." For me, those earthly desires that used to cause me unhappiness are now my sources of joy. The difference lies in my ability to use those desires to polish my life. Now, as it happens often in my career, if I am waiting on news in regard to a position, or a pilot, or a new series, I use my desire as fuel to help me chant with passion. This kind of chanting allows me to have great, valuable days and makes my desire my servant rather than my master. This is actually the most victorious experience in my life. I may wake up aching, needing a certain outcome, or worrying about my fate; but I have found again and again that if I chant for something I really want, something on which my happiness seems to hinge, I will experience the happiness before the desire manifests. Then that thing I wanted so much just becomes an extra bonus.

More important than any of this, though, is the development of what I first realized on that great day when I lost my car and my daughter's doll. I thought if I changed my pattern my daughter would be different and this would affect the generations to come. When we talk about that time in our lives, my daughter understands the difference. She knew how I lived. She saw her mother change what seemed unchangeable and win as a result. The cumulative effect of this one fact on my family's future seems unimaginable in size and scope. And that, apart from everything else, brings me profound joy.

The true beauty in life, for me, is the resilience of people, including my own. As I wrote the story of that period in my life, it occurred to me how much time I spent comparing myself to others, wishing my situation could be different, hoping things would change. I wish I could go back, tap myself on the shoulder and tell myself just how amazing it is to be on the planet, just the way we are.

Third Generation Rich,
First Generation Wealthy

Michael Riggins

Written by Zan Gaudioso

One man with courage makes a majority.

—Andrew Jackson

I WAS WHAT YOU WOULD CALL a third generation "businessman." My father was a gangster and a hustler, and so was my grandfather. I was born in Cincinnati, Ohio. My father had an IQ that was so high that he earned a physics degree in less than three years. My mother was an educator who believed that education was the key to everything. A serene and smart woman, she raised eight children. I was the youngest and second boy—in between us there were six girls. Being so far apart in age from my oldest brother, I seemed like the only boy in the family. With all my sisters and their friends, and the girls that my mother would take in to nurture and help, I was surrounded by girls. I lived with girls. I understood girls.

There was something in me that had my father convinced that I was born to be something special—maybe because I was smart like him, or maybe it was because, deep down, I always thought I would do something special, too. In either case, I would be groomed by a man who was wise, deep and blessed with a command of numbers that served him well in business but who would always look for his value outside of himself. I was on his path.

I was accepted to a college prep school. By day, I was one of the most popular kids on campus. I was winning academic awards, playing on all-star sports teams and being elected prom king. By night, I was learning how to beat the odds at cards by memorizing number combinations and how to properly treat "working women."

By the time I had graduated from Morehouse College in Atlanta, Georgia, I had a thriving business of my own. I had the world on a string, or so I thought. As for religion or spirituality, I didn't have a need for it. My father provided me with all the philosophy that I needed, or so I thought.

Religion was more of a joke than anything else. I had little regard for Christianity, the religion I was raised in. I would watch ministers pay a visit to my dad's business, his women, on Saturday night, before going off to preach their hellfire and brimstone on Sunday morning.

I moved to Los Angeles to become a "bigger fish." It was clear that the pond I was swimming in was way too small for my ambition. And I was right; it was happening for me in Los Angeles. I lived on the top floor of a luxury hotel in Westwood and making big money in many ways, including catering to Kuwaiti businessmen.

One day, I was working out at a private gym and next to me was a very "fine" looking woman. She was working that bike hard. I looked at her and said, "Girl, everything's gonna be just fine, all you have to do is have a little faith." It turns out that I was talking to a long-time member of the SGI-USA. She gave me an earful about faith and

Buddhism and before you knew it, I was invited to a Buddhist meeting—in the evening, no less. I thought, *That's just her way of asking me out.*

When I got to the meeting, I saw a bunch of shoes neatly lined up outside the door—I peeked in and saw people sitting on the floor! Here I was in an expensive suit and alligator shoes and they wanted me to leave them outside, come in and sit on the floor! I started to have serious second thoughts. Then Herbie Hancock, a famous jazz musician, came out to invite me in. I didn't know who he was and quite frankly, he wasn't dressed half as nice as me. What could he have that I could possibly want? I decided to go in anyway. The chanting I was hearing was somehow feeling good to me.

As the meeting went on, a little Japanese woman got up to speak. She wore a dress that came down past her knees— and I thought, *Do they even make those things anymore?* Then I started to listen to her. It was not so much what she was saying, but that little woman touched me in a profound way. Of all the stuff I did have, I saw in her something that I didn't. Tears streamed down my face. She gave me books and literature on Nichiren Buddhism. I took them home and read them all that night. I read "On Attaining Buddhahood" twice. It spoke about conscious choice and compassion. It was unbelievable. I also read the writings of the educator and second president of the Soka Gakkai, Josei Toda, and his disciple, SGI President Ikeda. In those two people I saw aspects of my father and my mother.

I called the woman from the gym and said, "I think

you've given me a real gold mine here." What I wasn't ready for was giving up my entire life, as I knew it—a world that was built on greed, usurious, indulgent behavior and running illegal practices. It would be a huge paradigm shift for me, realizing the importance of money in my life, but I felt deep down that it would be worth the trade-off.

I jumped into Buddhism with everything I had and I gave up most of my old life, much to the dismay of my girls and my pocket. I still had a bad free-basing habit, though. I was still getting my kicks the wrong way—from the outside in.

Old habits die hard, especially when they look like they hold the key to your happiness. I continued to chant more passionately to let go of the allure of my old life and to stop free-basing. I knew that I could never live the life I wanted if I kept grasping on to an illusion for my happiness. I chanted and I chanted.

On New Year's Day, even after making a strong determination to stop my habit, I went home and started smoking. While I was smoking I started coughing up blood, so much blood that it was dripping down my hand. With blood dripping from my right hand, and my pipe in my left, tears welled up in my eyes as I saw the obvious life and death choice right in front of me. At that moment I knew that I would never smoke again—and I haven't.

Everything would fall away except that which was real—the honor that my father taught me, the value and respect that my mother taught me and making the impossible possible that one little Japanese woman would continue to teach me.

Jobs were hard! I would always quit after that first check. Were they kidding? I was making in a week or two what I made in a nanosecond before!

But there was no denying that I had found my true joy and my passion, regardless of the job I was doing in life. I knew that Nichiren Buddhism held the answer to my happiness, which was a complete reversal from the life I had come from. I continued to chant.

As it turned out, a producer from a local Spanish television station approached me about playing a bailiff in the pilot for a new television series that he was producing, which I did! Weeks later, I learned that they loved me, they loved the pilot and they bought an initial thirteen episodes. This eventually led to me being on the top two daytime shows aired in thirty-six countries with millions of viewers!

I was invited to visit each of those countries where I appeared on talk shows and also met with and talked to dignitaries and thousands of children at elementary schools and hospitals to promote education and cultural understanding.

From not so humble beginnings to finding the true treasure of who I am through humility and grace; I have come full circle in my life. All the money, power and status that my father and grandfather amassed could not bring the happiness that they longed for and I was following in their footsteps, until I started practicing Buddhism. It has awakened me to the limitless potential and value of my life. I guess my father was right, I did grow up to be something very special—me.

DANCE 10, FEARS 3
TRISH GARLAND

If fear is cultivated it will become stronger,
if faith is cultivated it will achieve mastery.
—JOHN PAUL JONES

I WAS RAISED IN KANSAS in what you would call an average middle-class family. It veered a bit from the norm in that my father was an alcoholic—preferring to binge rather than sticking to a predictable schedule—who liked the thrill of trying to double his paycheck by gambling it. Mostly he lost. My mother was then burdened with the task of trying to make the remainder of the money feed four kids. She herself only had one dress and would forego the luxury of haircuts and instead wore her hair in a bun. At Christmas time we had a choice: we could either have one gift under the tree or we could wait for the after-Christmas sales and get twice as much. We, of course, opted for the latter.

Mom's thoughts around money, and her fear of never having enough, all rubbed off on her children, but in different ways. I became a saver, stashing whatever I could, while my siblings would spend. Her words were ever-present in my head: "Better save for a rainy day; you never know where your next paycheck will be coming from," and the ever popular, "A penny saved is a penny earned."

At fifteen, I won a Ford Foundation Scholarship to the

San Francisco Ballet. I was given one hundred dollars a month stipend. I saved half of it. Because I had chosen to be in the field of entertainment, it meant inconsistent work and an inconsistent paycheck. I was always panicking when I would finish one job, wondering if I would ever work again.

When I started practicing Nichiren Buddhism, I chanted to be in a successful Broadway musical. I had been in several shows but they never lasted long. I chanted for that to be different, never dreaming that I would be in a landmark musical. I landed the part of Judy in the original Broadway cast of *A Chorus Line*.

I had always believed in giving back to whomever or whatever was contributing to my well-being. For me that was definitely the SGI-USA. I gave what I could.

After my run in *A Chorus Line* was finished, I continued to perform in television and film but again with no real consistency. I would find myself waking up at three in the morning paralyzed with fear. I continued to have those same horrifying nightmares of never working again, but now it was even worse—I had a mortgage to pay. *Yikes*! The only way I could get back to sleep, or find any peace at all, would be to chant.

I did a guest shot on *Baywatch* and after that I got out of the business. I was unhappy playing these thankless roles. Now it was time to chant for "what's next" and further challenge my fears about money. I chanted to find my passion, for something that would utilize my talents and that would give me the kind of salary I was used to. An opportunity opened and it led me to my dream occupation. I became a Pilates instructor and eventually ended up owning my own studio.

My business was expanding and improving so much that, in accordance, I wanted to give more to the SGI-USA I cherished. My goal was to contribute more than I ever had each year for the next five years. I wanted to challenge myself. I felt that if I did, I would be free of my financial patterns that were born out of fear.

Every month, I would sock away whatever I could and lo and behold, I was meeting my goal! It was about a week before I was going to give my contribution to the SGI-USA, and I had taken the money out of the safe. I was trying to figure out if I should deposit it in my bank account or in my husband's. I had made the money but I thought if I put it in my husband's account that he too would benefit spiritually and emotionally from my donation. It was a thought that was still lurking from my past. There I was trying to provide for everyone, much like my mother used to. But in my case, I had a supportive, loving husband, consenting and agreeing with me every step of the way, a husband who stood on his own two feet as far as his financial well-being was concerned. It wasn't the broken, co-dependent squanderer, victim relationship of my parents. I knew I had to chant to become free from those beliefs that kept that world alive in my present. In my vacillation I simply shoved the money in a drawer in my closet.

That evening I went to a Buddhist meeting, and my husband went to a Lakers game. After we both got home and finally headed off toward the bedroom, the first thing we saw was broken glass and we thought a picture had fallen off the wall. As it turned out, a thief had thrown a heavy ceramic tile paver through our bedroom window. Among other things, he had stolen all the cash I had put in the drawer.

That evening, I could have beaten myself up for all the thoughts that caused me to put the money in a drawer instead of in the bank, but I didn't. Instead, I drew from my years of Buddhist practice and refused to be loyal to those beliefs of my past. In that moment, I knew I had broken through my wall of pain and fear, once and for all.

I made up my mind that my plan to contribute that specific amount of money would not be sabotaged. I would rely on faith and my original intent to give out of appreciation and my heart's desire. I didn't know how I would do it, but I trusted and I chanted. As it turned out, I was able, as planned, to give all the money I had originally set for myself as a goal. The money that had taken me almost a year to save was replaced and donated that month. How did I replace that money so fast? When I focused on what I could give from a place of abundance, not what I needed to save from a place of fear, the money appeared. As the second Soka Gakkai president Josei Toda said: "Even though your wallet may be empty, there is an abundance of money floating about in the world—it just hasn't come your way, that's all! But," he would continue, "if you accumulate good fortune, using it to 'drill a hole' into that vast reservoir of money and tap some for yourself, you will never have to be wanting."

My business continues to soar. The practices that my mother instilled in me were good practices, "a penny saved is a penny earned," but it was my Buddhist practice that allowed me to do it without fear, with appreciation, but most of all, with a joyous heart.

A New Step

Bob Hughes

Live with a dancing spirit. The stars in the heavens are dancing through space, the earth never ceases to spin. All life is dancing; the trees with the wind, the waves on the sea, the birds, the fish, all are performing their own dance of life. Every living thing is dancing, and you must keep dancing too, for the rest of your life.

—Daisaku Ikeda

WHEN I STARTED PRACTICING Nichiren Buddhism, it was only for a few months. I quit participating in many of the activities for a brief time because I thought what the people were doing was crazy. Little did I know that it was my crazy life just reflecting back at me. One thing I have learned from my Buddhist practice is that there's no one else out there—everything is about your life and how you perceive the world. This lesson would become crystal clear to me soon enough.

In the meantime, I was dancing in Bella Lewitzky's dance company and I loved it. I realized one of my life's dreams when a role in one of her ballets was created for me. Bella was one of the most influential and important people in my life, and the focus and discipline I would learn working with her would give me the foundation I would use throughout my life, for my life and for my Buddhist practice.

Then one summer, while I was working at my dad's steel company, my brother drove over my leg with a ten-ton forklift and the curtain closed for the final time on my life as a dancer. The doctors told me that they would have to amputate my lower leg. But because of my experience as a dancer, I knew the regenerative power of the body; and because of the great power of Nam-myoho-renge-kyo, I knew I could overcome anything if I chanted. This would be my opportunity to prove it to myself. I am after all a chanter. I believe in the power of chanting. I even believe that just thinking about chanting is powerful.

The surgeon gave me one week to change the color of my foot back to skin color. If I could do that then he would reconsider the amputation. So I did. I chanted mostly. I'd eat occasionally and watch David Letterman, but mostly I chanted. In less than a week, the color came back to my leg.

When you are a dancer, you dance. So when I became a Buddhist, I chanted. It required the same commitment— practicing the basics. Even if it doesn't make sense to you at the time, you practice. That's called faith. The unfolding is inevitable and has continually proven to be, if you practice with intention and commitment. I found that it is a process of simply peeling off layers to reveal something that's been there the whole time, that pre-existing condition of enlightenment. It is that place where all the power to create answers and all our limitless potential and value, reside. It is just waiting to be uncovered, and chanting Buddhist prayers did that for me.

But the question remained—what was I going to do now? I

was thirty years old with no degree, living in Washington, D.C., where it's all about degrees and communication skills. All my communication skills were essentially non-verbal—I was a dancer! I didn't know what I would do. The thing I wanted to do most in my life was to cultivate my own happiness and to help and chant for others to be happy too. But how would I parlay that into an actual living?

Once again, I knew that if I chanted I would uncover the solution. I chanted. Then it dawned on me that I was pretty good at "theatrical stuff." I had helped Bella's dance company in every phase of theater production, from the ground up—even when there weren't two nickels to rub together but there was still a show to put on. So I pulled out the phone book and started cold calling anyone who had anything to do with "theatrical stuff." Then I just followed the doors as they began to open. I paid attention.

Soon I got a job selling exhibits. I had never sold anything before in my life, but I understood space, and how to fill it. I continued to have a very active Buddhist practice, and at that point in my life I was committed to two things—selling exhibits and helping people better their lives. Other people's happiness was always very important to me, and I was beginning to understand why it became a giant doorway to my own happiness.

I gained more and more success as a salesman. But then I began suffering huge panic attacks, feeling as if I were going to have a heart attack. Just as with my foot injury, the pain—the emotional kind—would be my signal that something was wrong. Chanting brought out the healing at the time of my impending amputation, and I knew it would do the same for me now. There's one very important thing that I've learned from my Buddhist practice—pain is inevitable. Misery, however, is optional. I chanted slowly and deliberately in order to deal with the symptoms of the panic attacks, and then I was directed to a great therapist who helped me get to the core of my problem.

Therapy in conjunction with chanting was a winning combination for me. It was like the doctor/surgeon combination. Therapy helped me understand my suffering, while chanting helped me to restore my natural state of wellness.

It was at that point in my Buddhist practice that chanting stopped being external and it began to take up residence in my life as the fundamental truth. Suddenly, my health—mental, spiritual and physical—began to work in harmony to create my optimum healing and strength. I got to the core of my pain and really began to change my inner propensity for suffering and having accidents.

My inclination toward accidents would manifest almost immediately in disastrous ways. If I lied, I'd knock over a lamp, run into the wall or worse. On a deeper level, if I hated myself, I'd have an accident, crush a leg or attract an awful relationship. All that was about to change as I continued to practice Buddhism.

As I began to delve into my issues around money, career and relationships through chanting and therapy, I realized that I kept re-creating situations of financial instability. I thought, *I gotta learn why I have the need to continue to lose in these situations. Why is it so hard for me to make money? Be in a relationship?* Then I remembered Bella's advice, "Never take any short cut, never betray your own integrity and always do your best."

That advice, coupled with chanting brought up some important realizations. I realized that after so many years of selling "stuff," I still wasn't making any money. There was that pain again.

I started studying Buddhist principles on responsibility and, as a result, behaviors in my life that needed addressing started to surface. This awareness along with chanting gave way to action. That action was to pay back anyone I might have owed money to. Whether it was a nickel or thousands, friends or strangers, I would pay them back—to the tune of hundreds of thousands of dollars.

After I did that, the next natural course of action became obvious—I was to reinvent my company—and so I did. Then I began to make money, and I finally got the opportunity to do what I really love to do, contribute to the well-being of others. I decided to reconfigure my company as an Employee Stock Ownership Plan, where each employee would get the benefit of ownership, without having to take any money out of their own pockets. I also paid attention as the industry showed signs of change—it's those doors, again. I then came up with an invention that would serve the industry I was in. It would be the thing that would finally bring me security and financial peace of mind.

As the years passed, evidence of my healing became apparent and resulted in a marriage to a wonderful woman, success in my field and happiness that I would naturally extend to others. That's really what Buddhism is all about, finding your internal peace so that you can pass it on. Peace that begins in your heart, extends to your home, your community and eventually the world.

A commitment to Buddhism became a commitment to myself, as well as to others. It became my promise to honor and respect myself, to uncover the truth in all circumstances, that pre-existing enlightenment. My pain showed me the lessons I needed to learn: curiosity, courage and humility were the gateway to learning, and chanting was the underlying power that kept it all moving inevitably in a positive direction.

This journey is eternal. Making a commitment to pay attention to the doors that open along the way through my Buddhist practice has been my gift.

CHANGING POISON INTO MEDICINE
GREG CHAPMAN

Between stimulus and response, there is a space. In that space lies our freedom and power to choose our response. In our response lies our growth and freedom.
—VICTOR FRANKL

I T WAS MY MOTHER'S INFLUENCE and practice of Nichiren Buddhism that guided me toward this faith. My childhood wasn't what one might categorize as normal. My father was a famous baseball player for the Dodgers and my mother, a well-known model and dancer.

American icons such as Sammy Davis Jr., Elvis Presley and Frank Sinatra would frequent our house. We lived a *very* comfortable life and never concerned ourselves with finances. My parents divorced when I was twelve and as a result my mother was left to raise us children without the financial cushion to which we were accustomed. Those memories had such a profound effect on me that I developed a fear of money and financial loss, which I carried into my adulthood.

As an adult, I was trying to find my balance. I had two passions—music and Buddhism. I was very involved with SGI-USA. At the same time, I was equally busy traveling as a professional musician.

I wanted to establish a lucrative career for myself in an attempt to stave off my fear of losing everything, and I also wanted to nurture my spiritual side and fulfill my desire to contribute to a greater good. It became an incredible struggle between these two desires. Aside from the physical struggle of keeping up with both, emotionally I was overwrought by this deep longing and desire to abandon everything and just focus on Buddhism. Little did I realize how much the two desires were so integrally related. And little did I realize how much one was holding the answer for the healing of the other.

I maintained this state of duality for years. Although, I was profoundly successful by materialistic standards in the record industry, my fear of losing it all always lurked in the catacombs of my heart.

One year, something happened that would profoundly change the course of my life. My girlfriend's sister committed suicide in my house. That day will forever stand out among all others in my mind. Words on paper cannot even begin to convey how immensely this event would forever alter my life path.

Immediately, contemplation of life, death and my purpose gripped me hard. I had been attempting to introduce her to this Buddhist practice. I knew she had been depressed, but I never thought she would kill herself. I felt partially responsible for her death because I felt I had taken her depression too lightly. I also felt I had been cavalier about actually getting her to begin to practice. Maybe if I had been more persistent in getting her to chant, she would not have killed herself. I thought this for many, many months. It caused much guilt and suffering in my life, but it also was the main driving force for me to study in order to deepen my faith, learn and glean words of encouragement, and chant, study and chant. And that is all I did—for months. I began to focus on reduction and simplification. I was desperately seeking answers. Up until that point the art of negotiation had been my "Swiss-army knife" to all of life's difficulties. Yet here, negotiation had no place. I found myself in new territory where skills had no place.

Likewise, I had given up all my materialist gains. Everything I had built up and earned over the years—gone. What's more, I had no room in my heart to even care. I needed to focus on the deep onerous void I felt within.

For so long, the true meaning of the Buddhist teachings had eluded me. When I was younger, I knew that there was something very fundamental there, yet its personal meaning I did not understand. From that moment, I created a personal mission to unlock its meaning within my soul.

Then one night, I was reading two passages from Nichiren Daishonin's letters and I simply got it. It was almost as if he had written them to me. I realized that I was using my negotiation skills to get through life but I was not *living* life. I had built a wall between the world and myself. When my father left, I not only lost financial security and "stuff," I lost my father and mother, as I knew them. She was no longer happy and carefree. She was scared, lonely and burdened. I felt abandoned by my father who opted to live his life with other people. That's how it felt to me. The wall I built around me was to protect myself from that kind of pain from ever infiltrating my life again, but what it actually did was prevent me from participating in a fulfilling life. When my girlfriend's sister committed suicide in my home, a situation that I could not negotiate my way out of, the wall came crashing down.

These writings alone repositioned my view and vanquished my fears. I surmised from the passages I read that Buddhism exists so I, as a human, can "change poison into medicine." If this is true, then my path was clear. I would have to change my habits that were based on those childhood false beliefs in order to participate in life, be successful and most importantly, live a life that would allow me to enjoy my success. I realized that my own suffering was a necessary passage toward the truth of who I am and ultimately toward my true happiness. Likewise in business and in matters of money, I had to become like an alchemist. My fear would be transformed into joy, doubt into courage and selfishness into compassion.

Once I truly awakened my life based on Nichiren Daishonin's Buddhism, I was able to see this truth within myself and all fear, doubt and selfishness dissolved like dew on a blade of grass in the hot sun.

This is when I began to move through my life in a different way. I began by consciously chanting and living with gratitude and joy. I no longer feared failure in relationships or in business. At this point I had no idea what kind of career I wanted to have. I knew the record business was not an option for me anymore; I was done with that.

As I chanted every day I began to trust the process and just do things—whatever would come to mind, I would do. I went to computer conventions, read the *Wall Street*

Journal, searched the Internet for information, learning all I could about money, finances, the Internet, etc.

This went on for about three years; I don't even really remember how I made a living during that time. But my resolve was so strong that I somehow managed to pay my rent every month.

Through quirky twists of fate, synchronicity and chanting, and through relationships I began building based on trust, I formed a software company with a colleague. Years later, I am chairman and the major shareholder of three companies: a banking firm, a Web mail service and a holding company that develops real estate and incubates new technology companies—and I am happy.

In my past I was always trying to avoid problems and complications. I now look forward to any issue that will help me grow and better understand my life. That frightened child who had lost everything that he loved, and was so afraid to be happy again or to love again for fear that it would be taken from him, has grown into a man who does not have to negotiate or manipulate for happiness. I no longer have to subscribe to the fears of my past. Instead I can use them to create value, thanks to a profound Buddhist philosophy.

THE DUMB DUCKLING

DONNA LIANG

Strength does not come from physical capacity.
It comes from an indomitable will.
—MAHATMA GANDHI

MY MOM, DAD AND TWO older sisters all achieved great heights in their education and careers. I, however, was nicknamed the "Dumb Duckling." My family made light of it, but their jokes became the foundation of my lack of self-worth.

My parents had immigrated to Taiwan from China in the 1950s, and in 1975 we moved to the United States. My sisters and I were raised mostly by nannies so that my parents could focus on making money.

I was average in school. My sisters, meanwhile, broke every school record for academic achievement.

Out of desperation to move away from my parents, I graduated from high school at seventeen, found a job at a major hospital in Berkeley, California, and moved there within the month. I attended my first SGI-USA meeting shortly after I learned that my mother had breast cancer. Upon hearing people chant and recite prayers, I felt as if it was something I had been thirsting for all my life. I have not stopped practicing Nichiren Buddhism since that day.

After my mother died, every member of my family went into some form of depression, including me. My responsibilities as a Buddhist youth group leader to support others in their practice became my source of strength.

As I developed more confidence in my Buddhist practice, my family began mocking me for being so involved in Buddhism. Their ridicule brought back unwanted memories of all those jokes about me not being smart enough. I'll never forget one night in front of the Gohonzon when I made the strongest decision of my life—I would show my family my real strength and capability!

This wasn't easy. The childhood jokes had become recordings that played repeatedly in my head as I attempted to reach new heights.

When I finally graduated from college in 1992, I owed approximately fifty thousand dollars in loans. I had a degree in hospital management, but after two internships, I knew this wasn't the industry I wanted to work in.

Frustrated by my debt, at having taken so long to finish my degree and at being so far from my dream of success, I started a campaign to change my life, beginning by chanting with intensity. To save money, I moved in with my uncle. For the next few years, I lived in one of his extra rooms, a six-by-ten-foot room with a two-by-six-foot wooden table for a bed. I worked two jobs, starting at seven in the morning and ending at midnight.

Soon a woman who had her own software development company offered me a job. Having had the worst grades in math and with no computer science background, my chanting was all that enabled me, day after day, to learn what was necessary, no matter how difficult.

Because the new job was offered on a part-time trial basis, I was still working the other two jobs. So there I was juggling three jobs while also volunteering in my local Buddhist group.

I knew I could not let up. My endless nights chanting were not always filled with a sense of victory. I sometimes broke down in tears, asking myself, "What am I doing?"

The more I chanted, the more the pain and resentment from my childhood emerged, but I channeled this negativity into perseverance. I honestly don't think I could have continued without SGI President Ikeda's courageous example. When he was my age, he had the entire future of the SGI organization on his shoulders. Amid doubts, fear and tears, I read *A Youthful Diary*, Daisaku Ikeda's intimate account of his struggles as a young man. Visualizing the difficulties he endured and conquered inspired me to continue.

Before my trial was complete, I was hired full time as a systems analyst at the software company. My salary allowed me to quit the other two jobs. I continued to learn and work, and a little more than a year later, I was recruited by another company. I had reached a milestone. Not only was I on my way to a promising career but, more importantly, I had won over the years of self-doubt and recurring negative thoughts that once defined me. Rather than becoming a different person, I feel I have revealed potential I always had but which had been clouded over by my insecurities and negativity.

I decided at that time that I wanted to become even more

successful to prove not only to my family but also to myself that I could accomplish anything.

I spent the next few years improving my skills and going after bigger and more complex projects. By 1999, I was working for one of the most successful companies in the Silicon Valley. My company exceeded all expectations and made huge profits. Toward the end of 2004, the financial independence that I had chanted for was finally mine. At thirty-nine, I became the youngest person in my family to retire. It gave me the freedom to care for my father, who has Alzheimer's and other health problems. In addition, my sisters and I have become much closer.

Soon after, I started a company to generate support for socially important causes. My intention, much like SGI President Ikeda's, is to strive for world peace by propagating personal peace through personal happiness. Buddhism has helped me change my own destiny, which has changed the destiny of my family, and that has allowed me to reach out to the rest of my world. The dumb duckling turned into the swan that she always was. And it was not because somebody else finally said so; it was because of a deep and meaningful philosophy.

A Picture Perfect Mission

Glen Allison

The place to improve the world is first
in one's own heart and head and hands.
—Robert M. Pirsig

HAD I NOT ENCOUNTERED this practice of Nichiren Buddhism, I know without a doubt I would not be alive today. I was discouraged, homeless and hopeless. There wasn't much reason to keep living. I was hungry. My freelance photography business had been a failure. I was living in my van, and it was about to be repossessed.

What was left of my pride kept me from begging on the street. For food that evening, like most, I roamed the aisles of the local supermarket filling my grocery cart to the brim with all the best choices—not a penny in my pocket. Faking confidence, I marched through the store, all the while munching grapes, cheese and slices of bread from the packages I had opened. Hunger curbed, I nonchalantly parked the cart at the end of an aisle while I ostensibly went looking for more merchandise. Meanwhile, I slipped out the front door. I felt utterly defeated.

In the parking lot someone told me about Nam-myoho-renge-kyo. My eyes were puffed and I was choking back tears when she approached me. I had just stolen my dinner. I really hated myself. My practice of Buddhism began that night.

Even though I continued to live in my van for the next year, my life was soon bursting with confidence for the future. Day by day, the positive results from my Buddhist practice kept my spirits alive. My architectural photography business had never worked out before, but now assignments started to roll in. *The Los Angeles Times Magazine* featured one of my photos on the cover! Little did they know I was living in my van. The royalty check was mailed to my post office box.

Two weeks later I crashed my van on a Los Angeles freeway. I had been driving so fast that I ripped out seventeen fence posts of the center divider. I'd fallen asleep at the wheel. It wasn't until a few months later that I realized my life had, for some years, been possessed by a deep-seated suicidal tendency. Perhaps it had seemed the easiest way out during trying times.

My next brush with death shook me to the core.

I had always wanted to photograph the Albuquerque Hot Air Balloon Festival, so I left Los Angeles late one evening determined to keep driving until I got there. I chanted all the way. But in the middle of the night I succumbed to sleep. I had been driving a hundred miles an hour.

When I awoke, my car was wrapped around a roadside barricade—and around me. Miraculously, I hadn't suffered a scratch though my new car was completely demolished. Amidst the chaos, my mind had been calm for a brief moment, and it dawned on me how each successive incident had gotten so much worse. But by that time, my life had been awakened by Buddhism.

Tangled in my car, I screamed to the universe, "I don't want to die!" This had to end! No way would I continue being so irresponsible with my life. That behavior stopped in that moment.

My Buddhist practice launched me toward a fabulous new beginning. By no means was my life easy. Every time I attended a Buddhist meeting my spirits were somehow renewed no matter how hopeless the situation appeared at the moment; even if my photo gear was, once again, in the pawnshop. My photography business eventually exploded. Over time my photos appeared on the pages of *House Beautiful, House & Garden* and *Architectural Digest.* Soon my pictures were being published across Europe, in Japan—even in Moscow. In just a few years my images were being featured on magazine covers almost every month.

I kept chanting intensely. My personal life exploded to new heights, as well. I married a fantastic woman, a fellow Buddhist. She was a writer. Together we had dreams of traveling the globe pursuing our joint careers. We were able to land several international magazine assignments.

But soon another deep-seated propensity arose in my life—fast won success brought out arrogance that I had never recognized in myself.

It wasn't long before my self-centeredness destroyed my marriage and my photo business began a devastating downward spiral. I stopped practicing Buddhism and my happiness diminished. As a result I stopped contributing to the lives of others; I was only interested in myself. Not long thereafter I fell into deep misery. My famous clients seemed to disappear overnight. Eventually my landlord served me with an eviction notice and my car was repossessed. I was too arrogant to seek advice. Finally, my life reached bottom.

My years of Buddhist practice, however, had left an indelible imprint—I could always start anew. I kept recalling SGI President Ikeda's guidance to never give up—to rise like a phoenix from the ashes no matter what—regardless of limits. Eventually I found my way back to Buddhism, though I had to borrow a friend's bicycle to get to meetings. I devoted my efforts to help out in any way I could. Soon my life was enriched, once again.

In the following years my re-centered focus toward Buddhism manifested in a truly lighthearted spirit that thoroughly refreshed my life. As a result, my photography business flourished again. I earned one million dollars in three years. I had five full-time employees, and I owned an ultra-modern home.

Even though I was more than flush with money, I had never developed a real business approach to my finances; I was an "artist" and couldn't be sidetracked by those mundane concerns, especially when the money kept rolling in. When the real estate market crashed that year, my flourishing architectural photography business dried up and my "financial empire" collapsed soon thereafter. Within a year I found myself filing for bankruptcy. I lost everything. And, as shocking as it might seem, I eventually found myself living in my van, once again.

This time it was different. I was grounded in my faith. I got a pizza delivery job and I decided to be the absolute best pizza delivery boy that restaurant ever had—at age forty-five. As a result, my tips were huge. My Buddhist practice, as well as my Buddhist perspective, were resolute. I no longer lamented my lot in life. I was totally determined to turn poison into medicine. This seemingly low point would serve as a magnificent springboard for growth.

I was penniless and delivering pizza. On the surface anyone would have said that my dreams were frivolous. But my conviction was steadfast, and my Buddhist practice was daring.

Though it wasn't easy, during the next decade I found ways to continuously roam the globe and fulfill my dream as a traveling photographer. I circled the earth numerous times—homeless, this time by choice—for more than eight years with no permanent place of residence.

More than once in the beginning I found myself panhandling for food on the streets in faraway locales where I didn't speak the language. But I never gave up my dreams, and I never forgot about Nichiren Buddhism. I visited fellow SGI members all over the world and I sent back more than a dozen reports that were printed in our organization's newspaper, the *World Tribune.* Ultimately, I photographed one hundred and thirty-one countries in some of the most exotic regions of the earth. Early on my pictures had been accepted by the world's largest and most prestigious photo agency, Getty Images, and through their marketing efforts my travel photos have been published more than fifty thousand times in most of the world's leading travel magazines, including *National Geographic*. The royalties from licensing my images will continue for the rest of my life.

Previous losses have awakened me to how much I must challenge my self-centered nature and how not doing so in the past had caused difficult circumstances to arise. During my journeys, I made the decision to introduce one new lifelong friend to Buddhism in every country around the globe. I discovered my mission, and it was not just to become a great travel photographer—it was to contribute to peace in my own way.

My Buddhist practice has enabled my wildest personal dreams to come true. This awesome phrase, *Nam-myoho-renge-kyo*, has radically altered the course of my life. I am happy to be alive when once I wanted to die. I am now prepared, in whatever capacity, to challenge the future and help inspire others across the globe to do the same—one person at a time.

JOE'S STORY

JOE PEREZ

Written by Zan Gaudioso

A person of wisdom is not one who practices
Buddhism apart from worldly affairs but, rather,
one who thoroughly understands the principles
by which the world is governed.
—NICHIREN DAISHONIN

IN 1986 I LOST EVERYTHING. I mean everything—
except my faith, my Gohonzon and my understanding
wife. It was a real estate deal that took me down. I was a
vice president of a communications company and one of
the top 10 percent wage earners. I was at the top of my
game, and I thought I could do anything. I was wrong. I
cosigned on a real estate deal that went belly up, costing me
everything. It would become known as the time that I
would throw out my big ego and replace it with the deepest and most profound faith that I'd ever come to know.

Not knowing what to do, I sought advice from a trusted
Buddhist friend. He suggested I read and study the works
of inspiring men in Buddhism who have succeeded through
all kinds of adversity. He suggested that I put myself in their
shoes. I went home and read a book about the life of SGI
President Ikeda. Inspired by his life's journey, I decided to
go to Los Angeles.

With barely a nickel to my name, I kissed my wife, packed

173

my bags and headed for California to see if I could find work. I found a place to stay—the cheapest room in a motel—the dumpster room. I called it that because the huge dumpsters were right outside my window. The garbage trucks would come early in the morning to empty the bins. It was stinky and it was noisy, but for now it was home. I can tell you that it gave me a lot of enthusiasm to practice Nichiren Buddhism. I continued to read and I continued to chant.

Shortly thereafter, I met a man who soon became my friend. One day he came to me and said, "Joe, I have a friend in New York who needs help. His business partner has disappeared and he needs to find someone quick to help him with his business. Do you know anyone?" I wanted to jump at the opportunity right then and there, but my mind stopped me with all the reasons that I couldn't. I told him that I would think about it and get back to him.

I went home and chanted. This would be a great opportunity for me and it was more than just a job. I would be taking over someone's contract for business to help this man run a multi-lingual, nationwide company that advertises on the sides of buses. But how could I do it? Would I need to front the money to pay the crew? Pay for the trucks I would need? I just declared bankruptcy. I would never be able to get a loan. I didn't even know the terms of the deal. I was getting ahead of myself. I needed to chant. After chanting I knew that I had to ask him for the opportunity. My head was giving me all the reasons why it would be insane to ask for it, but every time I chanted, I would get the same answer—be true and be yourself. So I was.

When I next saw my friend and he asked me if I knew anyone who could help him, I enthusiastically offered, "How about me?" I told him everything. I was honest and I was myself—no pretenses, no hype. I came from my heart and it worked. His friend came out from New York to meet me, and soon I had documents in my hands to sign. He even offered to bankroll the payroll for me, and he advanced me the money that I would need to lease the trucks.

Years later, my friend would ask me how I could so confidently recommend myself for the position. I told him that, for one thing, I needed it, and for another, I knew I could do the job. I had already been a vice president of a company, and I had already been in charge of a large staff. I knew he needed both of those things. As far as employees were concerned, I was a Buddhist, and Buddhism and humanism are synonymous. People will respond and grow if they are treated with dignity and respect. It's the one thing they don't teach you in business school, but should—Buddhism!

I hired fourteen people and brought the donuts and made coffee. From the beginning I offered medical and dental plans for their families. After the first paycheck, without saying a word, I raised everyone's salary by fifty cents an hour. Only two of the guys came to me to tell me that they thought I had made a mistake. I immediately promoted them to supervisors. Everyone got two bonuses a year. It's the best investment any company can make in terms of productivity and loyalty. Now, with one hundred and twenty-seven employees, ten out of the original fourteen people I hired still work for me. And, the business that grossed

eighty thousand dollars a month has grown into a five million dollar a year company. It is now in seven major cities.

Today, I own three companies, including a charter air-
line. I have sat with heads of state, presidents and world
leaders. Because of my Cuban heritage, I have been instru-
mental in opening a dialogue between Fidel Castro and
Daisaku Ikeda and was brought to tears when I heard
President Ikeda tell Castro that "the Cuban people have a
right to be happy."

As a result of following President Ikeda's encouragement
to me to "chant for the happiness of your people and take
action," I live a life beyond my expectations. I share it with
my beautiful wife, Junko, of forty-five years, two great
kids, grandchildren, friends, colleagues and my remarkable
Buddhist community.

I know that all of this happened because of a fervent,
consistent Buddhist practice that could have never survived
if I were to settle for a big ego and a little life.

Oh, and by the way, I still bring the donuts and make
the coffee.

health

Everyone at some time suffers from illness in one form or another. The power of the Mystic Law enables us to bring forth strength to overcome the pain and suffering of sickness with courage and new determination.

—Daisaku Ikeda

THE CHIEF AIM OF MEDICINE in Nichiren Buddhism is to help individuals develop their natural self-healing powers by cultivating enlightenment through their Buddhist practice.

This view is gaining widespread recognition far beyond Buddhist practitioners. The World Health Organization Constitution reads, "Health is a state of complete physical, mental and social well-being and not merely the absence of disease or infirmity."

We are all human beings made of flesh and blood. It is an undeniable fact that no one can avoid illness at some time or another. But the roots of sickness exist in the depths of our being. From the viewpoint of Buddhism, illness cannot destroy our happiness (unless we allow it to do so) and, since the cause for illness is inherent within, the fundamental solution for it is also within. It is important to remember this. There is, then, no reason to be controlled by illness, no reason for it to fill us with suffering, fear or distress.

Nichiren Buddhism teaches us that we possess the power not only to transform the negative into a neutral state but also to go beyond that to achieve a positive state. We can overcome the suffering of sickness. Even the experience of sickness enriches our lives and makes them more worthwhile, providing the material for a great drama of fulfillment that unfolds day after day.

Helen Keller wrote in her autobiography, *The Story of My Life* that, "Everything has its wonders, even darkness and silence, and I learn whatever state I am in, therein to be content." Just as true happiness is not simply the absence of problems but an internal life-state that enables us to challenge any obstacles to happiness that come our way, health is not simply the absence of illness. Rather it is the state of being that enables us to overcome illness and the obstacles to our health. The important issue is whether we defeat sickness when it comes or whether sickness defeats us. Buddhism teaches us the source of wisdom and life force necessary for defeating illness. Because both health and illness exist as potentialities within us, we can make ourselves sick, and we can make ourselves well.

Locked within you are the great treasures of the Buddha nature—wisdom, compassion and courage. When you turn to this medicine cabinet, you truly are the Buddha in the mirror. In medical terms, every human being is both a pharmaceutical manufacturing plant—able to create the medicines needed to ward off illness—and a repository for all the positive human emotions that affect our ability to fight illness. The key to opening this repository? Chanting Nam-myoho-renge-kyo.

QUITTING WITH GRACE
CRAIG KIRSCH

We ordinary people can see neither our own eyelashes,
which are so close, nor the heavens in the distance.
Likewise, we do not see that the Buddha
exists in our own hearts.
—NICHIREN DAISHONIN

I STARTED PRACTICING NICHIREN BUDDHISM on a Tuesday. I remember because I went to my friend George's Tuesday night meeting; it was for beginners who wanted to learn about the practice. I had recently told another friend, Mike, that I was depressed, that I felt so absolutely hopeless. I was not happy with my job. I was not happy with my personal life, and I didn't know what to do. I felt trapped and helpless. So Mike suggested I go to the meeting at George's.

I remember being a little nervous but telling myself that I was just doing something new to see what it was like. "What was so difficult about that?" I understood the concept of taking action—you know pick a card, any card, but at least pick one! I also understood the concept of a body at rest tends to stay at rest and a body in motion tends to stay in motion. I even understood some of the basic tenets of Buddhism. So I put my "at rest" body in motion and dragged my depressed self to George's Tuesday meeting. For eight months after that, I don't think I missed a single Tuesday. You could say I went religiously, which is no small feat for a person who didn't believe in the concept of organized religion.

I immediately liked the ritual of the practice. It had a calming, yet invigorating effect. The following month, I went to my first discussion meeting. I remember that trying to follow the recitation of the prayers was like trying to jump into a game of Double Dutch—attempting to negotiate two jump ropes moving in opposite directions—when you've only just learned how to jump rope. But I also remember one of the members talking about how when she first started practicing she'd made a list of the goals she wanted to accomplish.

I knew right away what the first item on my list would be. Quit smoking. I wanted very badly to quit smoking. I wanted to change a lot of things in my life, but it was clear to me that the first thing I wanted to do was to quit smoking. The habit was consuming me, and try as I might, I could not quit. I had been smoking for the better part of twenty-two years, and in the last few years I felt like I had no control over the habit. So I made my list and then when I chanted, I focused on quitting smoking.

Practicing Buddhism made me think of my friend, Ben. Ben was an SGI-USA member, but I did not know it at the time. I did know he was a Buddhist because he used to say, "I'm a Buddhist, you know." So it was actually Ben who first introduced me to the practice, though never formally. It was also Ben who introduced me to George and Mike, though it wasn't until Ben died years later that I really got to know them. When Ben died, the three of us helped plan and conduct a celebration of his life at the SGI-USA Culture Center in Chicago.

One evening, I was doing my evening prayers, and I was really struggling and a bit frustrated. I wanted to go faster and make fewer mistakes.

I was sitting in my living room looking out at Lake Michigan doing evening prayers when suddenly, in my mind's eye, who should I see clear as day but Ben. The image I saw was of Ben reciting these prayers. It was an image that I had recorded in my mind years earlier. I went to pick Ben up one night to go out. He was just finishing his evening prayers, and I remember just sitting down and being silent.

Now, years later, here was this crystal clear image of Ben in my mind; how erect he sat while praying, how he clasped the Buddhist liturgy book, and how his elbows flared out from his sides like a bird's wings. I was thinking so much about Ben, it was almost as if he was there in the room with me. Then, I sat up straighter and let my elbows flare out like wings. When I did this, the words just started flying effortlessly out of my mouth. I kid you not. It was like I'd done the recitation a million times.

I started crying. I was still reciting those prayers, and I was still going at a faster, much smoother pace, but now I was crying. I was crying because I was happy that I could so clearly feel the presence of my old friend. It was like I could hear him saying again, "I'm a Buddhist, you know."

Soon after that, I realized that just chanting to quit smoking was not enough. I needed to take action. I went to see my doctor. I told him I was really frustrated because I had not been able to quit. He told me that if I were serious he would prescribe a mild antidepressant that other patients had used to help them quit smoking. I told him I was serious.

I took the pills as instructed for a week and set my quit date for May 21. During the first week I noticed that I didn't really like the way the pills made me feel. Sometimes they made me anxious. But I continued to take them for the week prior to my quit date, and I continued to chant. The main focus of my chanting was to quit smoking.

May 21 came, and when I got up to go to work that day something made me decide not to take the pills. I was hovering around my kitchen counter where the one hundred dollar prescription was, having my juice and my vitamins and wondering if I should follow the prescription's plan or my plan. I decided to follow my gut instinct; I didn't take the pills.

I went all day at work without a cigarette and without the aid of the drugs. I just kept thinking that all I wanted was to be on the other side of this habit. I just wanted one day without cigarettes. When I got home, I decided to go work out, and just before I left, I took the half pack of cigarettes that I still had in my jacket pocket and I soaked them in water and threw them in the trash. I remember thinking, *I can do this. It's not that hard. All I need is one day without cigarettes*. It was at that moment that I knew I could do it. I knew that not only could I make it through that day but that I could quit completely. What astonished me most was that it wasn't that difficult. In fact, I remember feeling calm and confident. It was like the non-smoking me had been there the whole time but only emerged on my quit date. *How strange*, I thought, *that I don't really have a craving for a cigarette.* How strange that deep inside there was this calm center of resolve that, I now realize, had been building up for months by chanting to quit smoking.

I haven't had a cigarette since that day in May. That September I officially joined the SGI-USA. Now I am focused on the other items on my list that I want for my life, and whenever I get frustrated I think about how practicing helped me quit smoking, something that had seemed impossible. I also think about how I feel something now that I didn't feel much before I started practicing—hope.

Sometimes too, when I'm reciting my evening prayers, I remind myself to sit up straight and let my elbows flare out like wings. After all, I'm a Buddhist, you know.

Japan, Asthma and the Power of Faith

Nancy Donohue

The ultimate measure of a man is not where he stands in
moments of comfort and convenience, but where he
stands at times of challenge and controversy.
—Martin Luther King Jr.

Since childhood, I had suffered from life-threatening asthma. I was sent to a convalescent home for young people for about a year when I was eight when the doctors told my parents there was nothing more they could do for me. The home was essentially a place where children were sent to die. I survived the first visit but was sent back for several more years when I was thirteen. When I was twelve, I weighed sixty-five pounds; it wasn't unusual for me to spend months at a time in the hospital.

In practicing Nichiren Buddhism and also utilizing a holistic nutritional approach, I was able not only to manage this condition but to overcome it. I made it to adulthood and I was no longer on medication. I could breathe easily—an essential life function that most people take for granted—without having to think about it. Then I was offered the opportunity to work as a copy editor and writer at the SGI headquarters editorial office in Japan.

I met with the bureau chief of the Tokyo office, who was in Santa Monica at the time. My next "job interview" was with SGI President Ikeda himself at a garden party in

Malibu. During the few moments I spent with him, he greeted me enthusiastically, shook my hand and said, "See you in Japan." I was so excited. I was going to live and work in Japan and to experience firsthand what it's like to practice Nichiren Buddhism in its country of origin.

To my surprise, however, I would have to face the asthma "devil" once again before boarding the plane. A month before I was to depart for Tokyo, it reared its ugly head with a vengeance. Suddenly, for no apparent reason, I was getting severe asthma attacks, and none of the usual holistic approaches worked. I didn't want to tell anyone because I knew it would jeopardize my chance to go to Japan. All I could do was rest, prepare for the trip and chant as much as I could. It's not easy to hide the fact that you can't breathe.

On the day of departure, with slow and careful steps, I made it on the plane. I took a lot of medication to keep myself together, to look normal when some of the editorial staff members warmly greeted me at Narita International Airport in Japan. They took me to my apartment, which was fully furnished and included a beautiful Buddhist altar. One of the female staff members told me that she would accompany me to the office the next morning. When they left, I collapsed from exhaustion, worried about how I'd make it through my first day.

The next day, after the warmest of welcomes, I settled down to work. There were deadlines to meet; the pressure was on. However, later on that morning, my condition suddenly deteriorated. I put my pencil down and quietly said, "I need to go the hospital." The editor in chief immediately arranged for three other staff members to take me to the hospital.

The hospital they took me to was administered by a physician who was also an SGI member. So were the nurses. I was treated with all kinds of medication; nevertheless, I remained in a state of panic. What if I were to die in Japan? With one of the nurse's admonishment, I snapped out of it. "This is about faith," she said. "Do you think this is just about your physical condition? This is a powerful circumstance for your growth. It's your *faith* that will enable you to overcome this life-and-death struggle, not doctors or medication. You have a mission, and you must survive." Since I could barely breathe, she encouraged me to chant silently. I was calmed by her words, and soon the medication began to work.

The next day, the gentleman who hired me came by to visit me. He told me that he met with President Ikeda to tell him that he would see to it that I was safely returned to the United States and that he would find someone to replace me. But President Ikeda said to him, "No, wait. Give Nancy the chance to face this challenge and change it."

Several days later I was back at work, feeling better and stronger, ready to take on the rigors of my job, learning more about Buddhism and experiencing life in Japan. I accumulated many great memories of practicing Buddhism and attending activities with other Japanese members. I traveled throughout Japan as part of my job as a copy editor and staff writer for SGI publications; I welcomed members from around the world.

On occasion, the asthma would resurface, especially during the winter and monsoon seasons, but it was manageable. However, one evening, about a year and a half later, I arrived home from work, feeling more breathless than usual. I didn't worry too much about it; I took some medication and used my inhaler. About an hour later, it developed into a full-blown asthma attack. It had become critical. I was not able to go to the local emergency room on my own, so I called for help. Two co-workers came to my apartment. They called for a taxi. It took me a long time to just walk down the stairs. The taxi driver drove the three of us to the Keio Hospital emergency room.

In the emergency room, I was given adrenalin, inhalation therapy and other medications. Nothing worked. I was lying down on one of the gurneys and thoughts of death began to take over my resolve to recover. I felt terrible about what the two young women were going through, who were determined to see me through this. We were all exhausted. Even a jaded New Yorker like myself was moved by their sincerity and concern. I no longer had the will to suppress the tears as they streamed down my face.

I can still see their faces as they stood by the gurney with their prayer beads draped over their hands, quietly chanting for me, overwhelmed by a feeling of helplessness. They kept saying to me, *"Gambatte, Nancy-san, gambatte, ne."* "Please don't give up Nancy; hang in there!" They were crying, too.

After several hours, there was still no improvement. Finally, the attending physician uttered these unforgettable words: "I'm sorry, but there's nothing more we can do for you." The same thing my parents were told so many years ago. I was overcome by the feeling of utter hopelessness. I was told to go home and try to relax; maybe the medication would take effect later on.

My friends and I returned to my apartment. I could tell that they were completely exhausted; I suggested that they go home, but they wouldn't hear of it. They would stay with me and rest there. I asked them to arrange my pillows on the futon and face me toward the Gohonzon so that I could prop myself up and chant silently. I decided that if I were meant to die that night, I would die facing the Gohonzon. My pulse was racing at about one hundred twenty beats per minute because of all the adrenalin. While the women slept, I focused completely on the Gohonzon and chanted Nam-myoho-renge-kyo about seventy times a minute—the same rate a normal heart would beat. It was a concerted effort to bring my heart rate down to normal. I forced myself to breathe normally. At first this took a lot of effort, but after a while, it became easier, and I was actually breathing more comfortably and my pulse slowed down to about seventy-five. I chanted this way until very early the next morning.

Later that day, I was admitted into the hospital—not for asthma—but for dehydration. I was released five days later, still feeling weak but able to resume work and activities with an even stronger determination for health than ever before. A week later, it was as if I were never ill.

What I learned from this experience had nothing to do with asthma. I realized that, when pushed to the limit, I could prevail and be victorious. Because of my memorable experience in Japan and my Buddhist practice, based on the power of faith, I realize that there is no limit to what I can accomplish.

I understood what true friendship is from the two young women who stayed by my side throughout the ordeal, and from so many others with whom I worked during my stay in Japan.

These days, whatever problem I encounter, I don't readily succumb to my naturally cynical outlook, and I don't feel discouraged for too long. I gather myself up and go forward, determined to embrace the present moment, unencumbered by any negativity. During moments of despair, I can still hear the bright and earnest voices of two young women from many years ago: *"Gambatte, Nancy-san, gambatte!"*

My Treasure

Arlaana Black

Life is a struggle with ourselves. It is a tug of war between moving forward and regressing, between happiness and unhappiness. Those short on willpower or self motivation should chant Nam-myoho-renge-kyo with conviction to become people of strong will who can tackle any problem with real seriousness and determination.

—Daisaku Ikeda

I DESPISED RELIGION. Like a dilettante Marxist, I was convinced it was the opiate of the masses, and it separated people, put them on unequal footing. So I rejected all, except witchcraft, which intrigued me, especially the dark side.

My connection to Nichiren Buddhism really began when I was in the seventh grade. I was required to write a ten-page term paper in order to skip the eighth grade. I chose to write about the caste system in India, an esoteric choice for my small school in East Flatbush, Brooklyn. When I was done, I was furious at a system that so blatantly denied people equality and freedom. Many years later someone introduced me to the teachings of Nichiren Daishonin, which embraced all people equally and was mystical-sounding enough to intrigue me to put witchcraft aside and pursue Buddhism.

I received incredible benefits early in my practice—a job in the recording industry, for which I wasn't even originally hired; getting into Columbia University's graduate program,

191

which I always assumed was for very intelligent kids from parents of substantial financial means, not a Brooklyn girl with a father who had little financial success as a garment industry employee, and a mother who was a bookkeeper.

The great benefit from my Buddhist practice, however, was yet to manifest. As a child I had been diagnosed with a heart murmur, and after several cardiac catheterizations, I was told at age twelve, that there was no longer any need for concern. The hole in my heart had naturally repaired itself.

However, at the age of thirty-two, and now years into my Buddhist practice, I had a chest X-ray as part of a standard medical procedure, and was told that my heart was quite enlarged. At first I found this somewhat humorous since about a month prior to this revelation, I was fired from a job for having "too big a heart," not being cutthroat enough. When I proceeded to get further tests, the surgeon told me that I had a "silent killer." He explained that once symptoms appear, the damage to the heart is irreversible. Typically, the person dies in his or her forties.

In an encouraging letter to one of his followers, Nichiren Daishonin explains, "The wonderful means of truly putting an end to the physical and spiritual obstacles of all living beings is none other than Nam-myoho-renge-kyo." If ever I had to put my full faith and confidence in my practice of Nichiren Buddhism, now was the moment. Undergoing life threatening open-heart surgery, as a perfectly healthy young woman, was indeed a test of my faith. But this was only the half of it.

At the same time I learned about my heart condition, my mother was simultaneously experiencing her thirteenth episode of bipolar disorder. She desperately needed hospitalization but had exhausted her medical insurance. My sister, just recently remarried, was about to leave for her honeymoon. I remember facing the Gohonzon and squeezing out whatever determination I could muster, crying out that Nam-myoho-renge-kyo had to work to repair my physical hole and my mother's spiritual hole.

Hours of chanting later, I went to my office, which at the time was at Columbia University. I opened the Columbia University directory and decided to call a special research facility at Columbia Presbyterian Hospital—the only one of its kind on the entire East Coast that had a government grant to study the correlation between heart problems and mental disorders. Since my mother had a pacemaker placed in her heart a year prior, she was a perfect candidate.

My sister and I brought my mother in for an interview. In my heart, however, I was afraid that there would be a long waiting list, since the study would only include ten patients. I continued to chant. After the interview, we learned that there was room for two more patients. My mother was immediately admitted. My sister grabbed me and with tears of joy repeatedly asked me how I was able to find such a facility. From the depths of my heart, I spontaneously responded, "I chanted!"

My sister left on her honeymoon, my mother was successfully placed in a wonderful hospital environment where she was treated extremely well, and now I could undergo open-heart surgery. The actual proof of my Buddhist practice continued to appear.

The day I was scheduled to be admitted, I was so frightened I wanted to cancel. But when I went to fill out the requisite admissions papers, the night admitting clerk had the words *Nam-myoho-renge-kyo* on her typewriter. I immediately felt reassured and encouraged. I decided that my real reason for having this surgery was to share this wonderful Buddhism with patients and hospital staff.

It seems strange to say that I actually had fun in the hospital, but I did. I had a wonderful roommate who kept me laughing, I loved the food and because I was talking about my Buddhist practice, I had tremendous enthusiasm and energy. I even recall an intern approaching me in disbelief that I had just undergone open-heart surgery, since I was in such high spirits a day after the surgery.

When my sister returned from her honeymoon she visited my mother, who was making wonderful progress. My sister told her that I had successfully undergone open-heart surgery. The words that came from my mother's mouth were Nam-myoho-renge-kyo. This from a Jewish woman who thought her daughter was strange to become a Buddhist.

When we were each released from our respective hospitals, my mother began her own Buddhist practice. She died of ovarian cancer a few years later, but she was able to conquer and overcome the deep mental anguish that caused her so much suffering. She found peace.

I learned that in my life I possessed a magnificent treasure in Nichiren Buddhism, and this treasure could never be denied me. Strangely enough, and yet not so strange at all, it is often called "the treasure of the heart."

Opening Doors

Bernadette Nicholson

To the weak, difficulty is a closed door. To the strong, however, it is a door waiting to be opened.

—ALMAFUERTE

WHEN I WAS IN LAW SCHOOL, I began to lose my eyesight and ability to walk. The cause was eventually diagnosed as multiple sclerosis, a devastating and progressive disease of the brain and spinal cord. Due to the great power of chanting, however, I regained my sight, ditched the wheelchair and graduated from law school with my class, winning a prestigious position with the Internal Revenue Service.

I eventually married a fellow Buddhist lawyer and moved to Northern California to run a family business. After five failed pregnancies, I became pregnant again. After almost losing this baby, too, my husband and I chanted for many hours with all our hearts for a healthy child. On August 5, Brandon was born healthy.

But our happiness gradually slipped away as Brandon suffered from a long list of health problems, including twenty-two ear infections by age two. He had three surgeries, including one in which he almost bled to death and another that removed a tumor from his neck. Then Brandon began having seizures after a drunk driver broadsided us. Brandon took seizure medication, and one doctor suggested a lobotomy. I cried, "Brandon, let's chant and beat this."

I shared with him SGI President Ikeda's encouragement to see ourselves winning every day. That's when Brandon, barely nine years old, started doing morning and evening prayers each day, visualizing himself defeating illness. Within one month, he was totally off medication and seizure-free.

Because I had received strong proof of the power of faith, I practiced even harder when the chips were down. I took Nichiren Daishonin's writings to heart. My standard became this passage from Nichiren's writings, "Whatever trouble occurs, regard it as no more than a dream."

When my marriage of seventeen years unexpectedly collapsed, I was devastated. Brandon and I were soon forced to leave home with no place to go. I didn't have time to be angry or frightened or to ask why. I said to myself, "You can't be defeated now. Not after all Brandon has been through!" So with the encouragement of my Buddhist friends and the wonderful support of fellow members, Brandon and I chanted an hour together every night. Despite my worsening health, I continued chanting until four in the morning, when it was time to wake Brandon for school. His commute was daunting—two trains, a bus and a mile walk. Within two weeks we moved into a nice apartment.

A couple of weeks later, I had to tell Brandon's school that I could no longer pay the tuition. We had painstakingly chosen this high school, and Brandon loved it. The school's admissions director responded in a note, "We cannot bear to not have you and Brandon as a part of our community, so we are going to fully fund him for the rest of the year." The next year, the school informed me that Brandon's entire high school education would be paid.

Buoyed by Nichiren Daishonin's words to "Regard your survival as wondrous . . . A coward cannot have any of his prayers answered," my courage and confidence in faith grew, along with my vast appreciation—appreciation for the people who had opened their hearts to us, for our own growth as human beings and for the encouragement and hope we had gained from our Buddhist practice.

Brandon went on to become student body president, co-editor of the student newspaper, student ambassador, captain and MVP of the basketball team, assistant girls' soccer coach and founder of the school's African American boy's mentoring program. He was soon inducted into the Cum Laude Society, graduated with honors and received the coveted Headmaster's Cup.

He enrolled at Princeton University with a full scholarship. Brandon will graduate from Princeton's Woodrow Wilson School of Public and International Affairs. He was accepted into two doctorial programs. It is rare to earn a doctorate straight from undergraduate school—usually a master's degree is required—but Brandon has proven that he can make the impossible possible with his Buddhist practice.

As for myself, I set a goal not to use the walker I'd been using for five years. I joined a group that pledged to chant an hour a day for world peace. It is so empowering to be united in prayer for the happiness of humankind. It was not long before I was all but free of the need for my walker. I only use it to help me carry things and for long walks. Soon I will not need it at all.

I have played many roles in my life—daughter, lawyer, wife, mother and friend. Today, I have carved out a new identity that does not depend on my profession or on being mobile, or on what others expect from me. Rather, it is based upon me, on the conviction that I am a Buddha and that my potential in this universe is unlimited.

I have learned, through my practice of Buddhism, that no obstacle is too great to overcome; and it is in the obstacles that I have found the gifts and it is in overcoming them that came the magnificent journey.

THAT'S NOT ALL FOLKS
SUSAN DAMANTE

*I choose hope because I feel a deep responsibility to do
what I believe I am obligated to do—to pass the world
on a better place than when I came into it.*
—DAVID KRIEGER

I CALL IT MY "THAT'S ALL FOLKS" moment. I was in
the intensive care unit and I was losing my life. And just
like at the end of a Warner Brothers cartoon, the circle of
light was closing.

Having suffered for eighteen years from what medical science has deemed an incurable bowel disease
called Crohn's disease, I was familiar with being in that
state. I had almost bled to death five times and had
recovered "miraculously" after each incident. But this
time felt different.

I started practicing Nichiren Buddhism after a very
enthusiastic woman approached me while I was loading
groceries into my car. She told me about chanting Nam-
myoho-renge-kyo. I was bulimic at the time and was buying food to eat and purge. I didn't realize that it would be
the greatest moment of my life; I just thought that she was
just another weirdo. Since I had been in Los Angeles a mere
six months I had been approached by anyone with a
cause—Scientologists, Hare Krishnas and born-again
Christians would zero in on me as if I were a target. Anyone

with a fervent desire to share their passion found me. For some reason, though, Nichiren Buddhism appealed to me so I decided to go to a meeting.

I started practicing because of two reasons: A woman was leading the meeting, and I had had it with all men, especially my father! Second, I felt like I was being given a tool that would help me change my life.

The leader taught that night about karma. I asked her, "Why should I chant these funny words to a piece of paper?" I was a positive thinker, and I was already "pretty happy." She asked me if there were situations in my life when I experienced feeling utterly stuck. When something would keep happening again and again, when you think to yourself, *Why am I here again? I am a good person, I try to be kind and positive, I haven't done anything wrong. Why I am back here suffering again?* I told her I could think of thousands of times when that was the case. She explained, "This is what Nichiren Buddhism explains as karma, or the law of cause and effect. This is why you chant funny words to that piece of paper. You can transform your karma through chanting. You can try it and you will see for yourself." I did.

A turning point came while I was in an acting class. I developed a blockage in my intestines that rendered me incapacitated. I was rushed to the hospital and while in the emergency room I did my evening prayers, out loud, even though it felt like someone was jamming a knife into my midsection. The realization I suddenly had was a deep understanding that I was not a victim of circumstances. I could rely on no one else, not the hospital, not my doctor, not medicine—just me. The next morning I woke up knowing that something had changed. My doctor, in his ironic fashion, told me that they could not find the cause of the bleeding. If I ate something, and then was able to go to the bathroom, I could go home the next day. And so I did.

The next day, I was chanting with gratitude and appreciation and knew that the experience I just had was serving a deep purpose. It was teaching me that I must no longer hold on to an old belief system that portrayed me as a flawed sinner. Nichiren Buddhism teaches that we are all Buddhas, and we all have the potential for enlightenment in our lives.

I realized that I had been living life with what I now call a "low moan." Every time something positive would be said to me, or every time I would have a winning moment, I would negate it unconsciously. That day, I became *very* aware of that belief system.

I would have to make a strong resolve to overcome begrudging my life and holding grudges against others— men and fathers, too. I realized that I had been trained in my life to suppress my emotions, including anger and asking for help, and I knew that it was killing me inside.

It took years of what I called attending the "University of Susan" to arrive at the night before the "That's All Folks" moment. During that time, I formed a motto for myself, "Say yes with purpose; say no with conviction."

After that, I volunteered to take a leadership role in the SGI-USA. By that time I was a talent manager for both my daughters' acting careers and I was on location a lot. But I wanted my practice to help others. I wanted to uplift and inspire. So one night, I stood up and announced to all of the members that I would take the position.

The next day, I was bleeding internally and close to death. It was definitely a test of faith.

That day was busy. There were auditions, school, the girls, homework and meetings. I was on my way to a meeting for new leaders. My daughter was battling for my time, insisting I stay home to help her with her homework. We argued. Before I left the house, I went to the bathroom and was faced with an entire bowl filled with blood. I can only describe the next several hours as a battle between "the old me" and "the emerging of the new me." My first reaction was the old me, "Oh, it must only be a hemorrhoid. I'm probably fine. I'd better get to the meeting."

Upon arriving at the community center, I passed another bowl of blood. This time the wisdom inside me was loud and clear: "Call the doctor, *now*!"

I couldn't even chant in the car, I was so enraged with this happening again. I felt utterly victimized. Why me?

When we arrived at the emergency room, I spoke to my family. My husband stayed home with the girls, because they were freaking out. It was the first time my younger daughter realized that my life was in danger, and my older daughter was really upset because we had fought before I left. I spoke to them and tried to reassure them.

My doctor soon returned and said he wanted to admit me. I was really shocked. I said, "Admit me? Really? I don't feel that bad, even though I passed some blood." Old Susan strikes again! My doctor knew me eleven years by then, so he grabbed my hand and said, "Susan, healthy people can see blood at the tip of their finger if they squeeze it. Look at *yours*!" My hand was completely white.

It was almost midnight and my husband had asked the hospital to leave the phone off the hook so he and the girls could stay connected.

While prepping me for surgery they had to take my orthostatic blood pressure, which requires the patient to stand, then lie down while being tested. At that moment, it felt as if a dam had burst inside of me and blood poured out everywhere. I grabbed the phone and shouted to my husband, "Start chanting!" I could hear all three of them chanting vigorously!

"That's All Folks" began and when it was about to go dark, I suddenly saw and heard all of the faces of the SGI members from the night before, all of my loved ones and friends and family. They were all there repeating the words, "You can't die. Your life is for the sake of others." Suddenly, the circle opened, and I knew something had changed—a cycle had come to an end.

The next morning my doctor came in to see me, and in his puzzled way said: "Well, we couldn't find the cause of all that bleeding. But if you eat and pass your food, I guess you can go home."

That was the last time I saw Crohn's Disease. It was gone. Completely.

For more than twelve years, I have been disease free. It

took me about five years to realize the revitalization that my body was undergoing. I keep saying, "I'm reversing so much that soon I'm going to be a baby again!"

Has my life been for the sake of others? Yes, but not as a victim or martyr, but as someone full of appreciation for my life and my precious faith. Each day is a gift, and I practice so that I can uncover more of my own inherent inner wisdom. I continue to align myself with a Buddhist philosophy that aims to awaken people to their limitless potential and value. I will never give up and will encourage others to do the same because "That's *Not* All Folks!"

HAPPINESS

CATHY ROBINSON

For it is not joy that makes us grateful;
it is gratitude that makes us joyful.
—DAVID STEINDL-RAST

AFTER TEN YEARS IN A wonderful marriage, my husband and I decided to have a child, but I couldn't get pregnant. We went to fertility doctors, I took shots and I tried artificial insemination, to no avail. To want a child and be disappointed month after month, year after year, was extremely painful. It brought up feelings of inadequacy.

During this whole period, my husband developed juvenile (Type 1) diabetes. He wound up in the hospital because we didn't know that he had the disease. He couldn't work for a while, and I wasn't making a lot of money, so we went into major debt. But I was always able to rejuvenate hope though chanting.

After six years of trying unsuccessfully to get pregnant, I decided to go to Japan for a Buddhist training course, as I had done once before when I needed spiritual sustenance. I started putting a little bit of money aside every week, determined that both my husband and I would go. I managed to save enough for the trip.

In Japan, we met with a longtime member who shared an experience with us. He told us that he had once had severe throat cancer and had been given six months to live. He refused to accept that diagnosis and proceeded to chant seven hours a day for six months. It was now seven years later and he was still alive and chanting three hours a day. He told me that I needed to have 100 percent faith, 100 percent confidence and that even though it was important to have doctors, I couldn't let them, or anyone sway me. I had to know that this could happen for me and chant with the same conviction that he had sustained . He gave me a gift of beads and a scarf for my unborn baby, and we returned home.

I chanted and reached a point where I realized that no matter what, I could be happy. I did get pregnant, but I lost that baby. I had an ectopic pregnancy. I was still encouraged, though, because now at least I knew I *could* get pregnant—without any drugs or artificial means but just from chanting with deep confidence. Six months later, I got pregnant again and was able to carry this baby to term.

Our son is a wonderful, incredible boy. Being a mother has been the greatest experience of my life. So much of what I learned from my past has helped me become a better mother.

When my son was eight, I began to develop a tremendous pain in my shoulder and went to an orthopedist. An MRI revealed a tumor on my spine, and it had to be removed immediately.

After the surgery, I was put in a brace from my neck to my waist. I would have to be in that brace for four months. While lying in the hospital bed, chanting, I had a deep experience. I understood why I needed to go through this to change my life and my destiny.

I was forty-eight at the time. My mother was forty-eight when she tried to kill herself by jumping out of a window. She survived the fall but had to be put in a cast from her neck to her waist. Here I was, at the same age, also confined from neck to waist. She and I had both gone through the same experience. Even though they were for different reasons, both experiences could have ended our lives at forty-eight.

A year after that suicide attempt, my mother killed herself with pills. I made a pledge to change my family's destructive propensity. I was determined. According to Buddhism, it is possible to affect your family seven generations behind you and seven generations ahead of you. Whatever I needed to do to accomplish that, I was prepared to do it. As I lay there in the hospital with that brace on, I knew that I was already changing things. I was changing it physically, emotionally and mentally. I felt free, even though I was in a physical prison.

The tumor turned out to be cancerous. I had lymphoma. I was scared, but I chanted, and a lot of my Buddhist friends came over to chant with me. I had to lie on my couch and roll off to get up. I couldn't take a shower without someone helping me. I couldn't drive or take care of my son very well.

Friends and people in the community came with food and gifts and even wanted to clean my house for me. I couldn't believe how fortunate I had become. I knew by these changes in my environment that I had changed my life and my familial patterns.

When my parents died, I was alone. I had no one. Now I had so many people supporting me that I thought my heart would burst with gratitude.

Through all that, I was still extremely frightened with the diagnosis of cancer. I sought out the counsel of a Buddhist friend who had known me since the beginning of my practice. I said, "I feel like falling apart, I feel like my hope is ebbing. I was so strong during the surgery, but now knowing the tumor is cancerous, I don't know if I can raise my hope again."

He said, "Cathy, all your life you have been very emotional, but underneath that emotion you have always been so strong. All the experiences that you've had with Buddhism have brought you to today. You can't be swayed by your emotions, that's just the surface. The strength that will propel you over this hurdle is inside you." That was an important concept for me to understand: the notion that being emotional doesn't mean you're not strong or you can't overcome adversity.

After the first chemotherapy treatment, I lost all my hair. I was devastated. Five minutes after my hair fell out, the wife of my Buddhist friend just happened to visit me. She walked in the door and I yelled, "My hair came out!" and I started crying.

She suggested we chant. She chanted so intensely that I came out of the depths of despair, feeling completely confidant in the future and in my ability to be happy.

The treatments continued for six months, and all signs of the cancer disappeared. Not only had I overcome the cancer, I had also developed much more confidence in the way my life was unfolding. I felt everything was happening the way it should, in the right order and the best outcome was assured. I understood how each moment is meant to help you change and make your life even better. I really got it for the first time that there wasn't anything in life that had to be negative. It could all be turned into something positive and wonderful.

Shortly thereafter, I received a call from a good friend of mine who asked me to chant with a friend of hers, who had just been diagnosed with cancer. We went over to her house to encourage her, and I shared my experience about my cancer with her. This woman wasn't a Buddhist but she said she wanted to try chanting, so we began.

In the middle of this, her daughter came downstairs and said the World Trade Center had just been hit. I took a deep breath because my husband worked in the World Trade Center. I said, "We need to keep chanting." For a second, I was ready to fall apart, but instead, I continued to chant. I knew I couldn't do anything for my husband at the moment except to chant. As we did, I felt a sense of peace well up inside of me. I was confident that he would be OK and so would our family, and I felt it deeply.

As I drove home, the fear came up again. I chanted the whole way that my husband would be safe and that nothing would happen to him. When I got home, I turned on my answering machine and heard my husband yelling, "I'm out! I'm out!"

Even before September 11, I felt that world peace could

only be achieved through respecting each other's differences. I am so blessed to belong to an organization that believes in creating value in the world by creating value and peace in your own life; and I belong to a religion that embraces every person of every religion, and seeks to create harmony through dialogue and understanding. Buddhism continues to serve me, and my world, very well.

Wanting a Cookie
Nicolas T. McCraith

Illness gives rise to the resolve to attain the way.
—Nichiren Daishonin

I WEIGHED THREE HUNDRED FIFTY POUNDS when I started practicing Nichiren Buddhism. The first time I ever went to the community center, the speaker talked about chanting for world peace and chanting for a cookie. As a heavy person, I understood someone chanting for a cookie.

I wasn't always obese, though. I started really gaining weight after I tore some major ligaments and my meniscus in my right knee, on the way to playing hockey. I was overweight, but that accident immobilized me. I could barely move. By the time I had my knee surgery I was much heavier, and after my surgery I was bedridden for weeks. To complicate matters, doctors found a massive blood clot in my knee that, were it to travel to my heart, lungs or brain, could kill me. So the doctor put me on daily shots in the stomach, and then on a blood thinner, warning that I'd be on it for life. I would not be able to travel by plane, something I had wanted to do. My doctor encouraged me to lose weight, but it looked hopeless. At twenty-three, my weight was rising and I couldn't exercise because of my knee; but not losing weight was causing more harm to my knee and increasing my chances of harm from blood clots. It was a Catch-22.

When I started practicing Buddhism, I never thought to chant for my health. I chanted to become calmer and less easily incited to anger. My family quickly noticed a positive difference in me in that area. At a Buddhist meeting a friend talked to me about how he chanted to improve the pain in his arm. "You can chant for health," he said.

Unsuccessful with diets, I determined that as of the New Year, I would lose weight and I'd get healthy. And I'd get a girlfriend! In the evenings I chanted to lose weight; in the mornings I chanted to get healthy and meet girls. Throughout the day, whenever I felt hungry, I'd chant to forget my hunger. Chanting helped me focus on my determination and helped me curb my cravings. Chanting also gave me the strength to stick to a healthier diet.

Through this regimen of diet and determination, girded with a lot of prayer, I lost one hundred pounds in eight months. Moreover, my doctor recently told me that the blood clot was gone, thanks to my weight loss, and he took me off of the blood thinner. Overjoyed, I immediately flew to New York with my sister and cousin. To date, I have lost nearly one hundred fifty pounds. A person really can chant for anything they want! In place of that one hundred fifty pounds of lost fat, I gained the sense of how powerful Nichiren Buddhism is. I have taken a major hurdle in my life and created immense value where there was only fear and a grim outlook. I now know how to face my problems. I now know how to be successful in my life.

As SGI President Ikeda writes in the book *On Being Human*: "Sickness helps people pioneer a more fulfilled way of living by reflecting on the meaning and dignity of life. The very process of overcoming illness tempers body and mind and enables us to create a still broader equilibrium. This is the source of the radiance of good health."

At twenty-five years old and one hundred fifty pounds lighter and healthier, I understand through chanting Nam-myoho-renge-kyo that the way to solving anything in my life, the way to my enlightenment, is within me, and not in a cookie.

MICHAI

VALENTINE A. ILLIDGE

Life is either a daring adventure or nothing.
—HELEN KELLER

SHE WAS BORN ON THE FIRST day of spring in New York, hardly causing me any pain. New York is a city that offers much to do, so much adventure for a young life, but for Michai it would be different. She would be diagnosed with muscular dystrophy at a young age.

Muscular dystrophy is a genetic disease characterized by progressive weakness and degeneration of the skeletal muscles that control movement. There are different variations of the disease, the worst of which projects a life span of not much more than twenty years. I lost my youngest son, David, when he was only twenty-nine.

When Michai decided to practice Nichiren Buddhism with the vigor and devotion that she lends to the rest of her life, I knew her prognosis would be different. I knew that she would make the impossible possible.

Michai has shown throughout her life that her erudite nature and keen sense of caring for others wins friends and protects her interests, which are many. Her smile can light up a room, and she can tantalize you with her eyes. That's why when she finally told us that it was time for her to be in a wheelchair, our world seemed to cave in on us. She, however, remained undaunted. Quite the contrary, she was soon rescued by a wheelchair that gave her stability. After experiencing so many unavoidable falls, it gave her a measure of comfort, and it would soon become her legs. I have gained so much from her precious life: a life of promise that blossomed into a life of love with conscious devotion to itself.

In the crowded streets of New York, where neither car, nor taxi would hardly stop for a person, let alone one who was wheelchair bound, life was hell! Thanks to the school bus—and Michai's decision to see beyond the city block through her love of books—there were no barriers for her, and her life evolved.

She has never lost her sense of herself, because it was always nurtured with love and prayers. In her pink polka dot painted room, Michai never stopped chanting for answers. She was consoled that even without the strength of her legs, she had the strength of her faith, which gave her life!

She went to her school prom looking like an angel in a soft pink lace gown. She was growing up so fast. She graduated with a 92 percent academic average and set her sights on California, more specifically, the University of California–Berkeley.

She hardly talked on the plane. I thought, *Did my child lose her mind wanting to do this?* She found her footing, though, and after a couple of weeks she began to enjoy her newfound freedom. She was left in the hands of a very capable female attendant, who was also a Buddhist. She learned how to trust and release her faith and became stronger. Michai and her attendant got along famously, and they cherished each other.

Michai and I talked often. She loved the beautiful spring-like weather that allowed her to challenge herself like never before. She was so protected that even during the 1989 earthquake, three thousand miles away from home, trapped on the campus grounds while mounting a ramp to her dorm, she was safe. She never complained about anything!

One day she said to me, "Ma, if I do well this semester I would like to study abroad." I gasped for air. Could I really be hearing this again? Was she kidding? Michai was pursuing Mideastern Studies, and since she had also studied Arabic and Hebrew in high school, she thought that going to Egypt would be great!

"Child, how can you sit there and tell me that you want to go to Egypt? You barely just got to California!" After I thought about it and prayed about it, I consented. I didn't want to hold her back. Even though counselors were trying to dissuade her and I had my doubts, no one could really discourage her. Everyone knew that Michai could move mountains.

I chanted for her protection and happiness, and on a foggy summer morning right after sunrise, three of her friends, her attendant and I took her to the airport to catch a plane to Egypt. Michai was again taciturn. Perhaps she was scared to be embarking on this adventure, but she trusted her decision, her gut and her faith.

My child went to Cairo, where she studied for ten months. She befriended the Nile, smiled at the Sphinx and was awed by the Pyramids. What a dream come true! She became the first handicapped student sent by Berkeley to study at the American University in Cairo.

While in Cairo, her boyfriend, Nicholas, flew to be by her side after an earthquake hit the land. They eloped and were married in Egypt.

She graduated from the University of California–Berkeley, with a double major, one in Mideastern Studies, the other in Women's Studies. She has shown me, through her example, the truth of all aspects of Nichiren Buddhism we practice. She has deepened my own devotion.

Michai has been happily married for eleven years and has founded "Glad To Be Here," an organization whose intention is to empower women with physical disabilities to lead full and independent lives.

Through chanting Nam-myoho-renge-kyo, my child has transcended her potentially fatal diagnosis and turned it into her strength and inspiration.

Her life, precious to many, has grown in spite of the odds and because of her faith; and that has given rise to her ability to make the impossible possible.

6

relationships

The heart of one person moves another's.
—DAISAKU IKEDA

OUR INTERACTION WITH OTHERS mirrors the inner realm of our own lives. It is here that our lack of wisdom or compassion is starkly revealed. It is here that arrogance and cowardice are glaringly exposed. For these reasons, it's often easier to avoid interaction with others rather than trigger these less desirable sides of our character.

We can quit our job or dump a love interest just so many times before we find ourselves gradually becoming chronically unemployed and terminally lonely. Avoiding the problems of human interaction is to succumb to more negative influences. It is to allow ourselves to wallow in the muck and mire of our own lesser self. And that's not happiness.

There is a great line from the movie *As Good As It Gets* starring Helen Hunt and Jack Nicholson that says it best.

Nicholson plays a self-absorbed curmudgeon who has unexpectedly fallen for the younger Hunt. They find themselves on a date, of sorts, in a nice restaurant in Baltimore. She finally demands in exasperation that he stop talking about himself and say something complimentary to her or she's going to walk out of his life. This is his one shot at touching her heart. But again he begins talking about his problems, his way of life, his priorities. She gets up to leave when finally he says, "You make me want to be a better man." At first she hears only that it's something else about him. But then realizes the compliment. She has become important enough to him for him to want to change himself for the better in order to keep her.

Relationships that matter enough for us to wish to become better people are a crucible for inner transformation, lasting happiness and the cornerstone of world peace.

FATHERS AND SONS
ROBERT DIXON

*As deeply as we have reached for the stars we must
delve into our hearts and find that universal connection
that makes us all one—then will inner peace be forged
in order to create peace in our world. We face an
unparalleled moment of possibility.*
—AARON SORKIN

MY FATHER'S NAME WAS Ray A. Dixon, and his death represented a turning point for me. It was both a sadness and a great victory in my life. Let me tell you about him.

Dad was a child of the great depression. At the age of ten, he lost his mother to illness, and his father "loaned" him to a farmer outside of town for additional labor. He had a difficult young life, and his schooling during this period was dictated by the amount of chores he had to do on the farm. If there was a lot to do, he didn't get to go to school. Although he was quite intelligent, being raised as a labor commodity—and without kindness—deeply shaped his personality, his beliefs and his life. He grew up to be a silent and angry man whose main criterion for human worth was the amount of work one could do in a day.

When I was born, although my father loved me, he was neither taught nor had the mental or emotional capacity to know how to extend love, pride or any sense of approval to his only son. His bleak, joyless childhood extended into his own family. Making matters worse, his only sense of artificial happiness, his only solace, came from drinking. This, in turn, made my mother angry and ashamed and further fed into a contentious family environment.

I was well on my way to continuing a family legacy based on pain and disappointment until those patterns were interrupted for good. I started practicing Nichiren Buddhism. I was seventeen years old and my life was about to take a radically different turn than what one would expect from my beginnings. Suddenly, I saw a grander world than I would have ever known being born the son of a troubled family. It was a vision bigger than any that was ever presented in my house.

Much to my parent's consternation, I devoted my life to this Buddhist practice and activities. It was beyond my father's comprehension why I would be spending my time in an organization that wouldn't contribute to my future, as he saw it. But I saw myself as part of the twenty-five-hundred-year history of Buddhism, a teaching with tremendous respect for life, instead of being defined by my father's pain and my mother's anger.

Buddhism would begin to resolve my own pain and anger and feeling of worthlessness by fundamentally changing the way I felt about myself from the inside out. My pride and self-esteem would come from the knowledge that I was an enlightened being with infinite potential. Suddenly and indescribably, my personal happiness would be born out of that understanding.

Buddhism allowed me to see the bigger picture of my life, my father's life and our relationship. My inclination to blame and live the unhappy consequences as a result became opportunities for me to grow, to change and to learn how to rewrite my own legacy. The buck would stop here. The chain of anger, unhappiness and lack of love that gave way to an inability to approve and value another human being would be transmuted through my diligent practice of Buddhism.

As my compassion grew, my anger melted and I came to appreciate the things my father did in the face of his adversity. According to my uncle, my father's brother, the painful father-and-son relationships had been carried forth for several generations and I was the first one to make a dent in it being any other way.

Practicing Buddhism and changing one's life so profoundly, human revolution as it is called, penetrates all aspects of one's life, and so it happened with my father. One year, in an unprecedented decision, he opted to attend his first family reunion in Arkansas, and he invited me to come along.

I was producing a show in Chicago at the time, but I immediately hopped on a plane and flew to Texas to meet up with my father and uncle. My father had already flown to Texas from California, where he lived. The plan was to pick up my uncle in Texas and then the three of us would drive to Arkansas for the reunion. I had never really met anyone from my father's side of the family, not even the uncle I was about to meet. I felt sure that this trip would continue the unraveling I had started, the unraveling of my family's painful dysfunction. And in fact, that's exactly what it would be, but not in the way I had envisioned. Before we left Texas, my father had a stroke.

Fortunately, he survived. I spent five days by his side in Texas and after he was well enough to move, I was with him for two more weeks in a hospital in California. The stroke had left some weakness, but his capacity for understanding and his mental acuity were not diminished. That was our gift in the time we spent together. We were brought closer than ever before.

Because of my Buddhist practice, I had gained the courage and clarity to say things to him without blame and without guile. I was able to express my gratitude for how much he was able to do for us—my sister, my mother and me. I told him that he was a good father, doing the best he could, and I told him that I loved him.

Throughout the days, I read to him from Daisaku Ikeda's book *Unlocking The Mysteries of Birth & Death*. It gave him solace and an understanding and appreciation of why I had dedicated my life to Buddhism.

Our time together gave my father more courage than I had ever seen in him before. It gave him the courage to tell me that he loved me, and it gave him the courage to die. Ten minutes after I stepped out of his room he slipped away, peacefully and secure in our relationship.

I will be eternally grateful that I was able to culminate a lifetime of learning, through a powerful and compassionate Buddhist practice, by communicating with my father in such a profound and loving way. Together we broke through a destructive family tradition and ended the chain of pain.

When I watch the way my youngest son is raising his daughter, I see evidence of our work. When I see the dignity and respect with which my eldest son treats his employees, I see evidence of our work. And when I look into the eyes of both my sons and tell them how much I love them and how proud I am of them, I see evidence of our work.

About A.J.

Joseph Malone

If each of us sweeps in front of our own steps,
the whole world would be clean.
—Johann Wolfgang von Goethe

MY WIFE, NANCI, AND I married twenty-three years ago after dating for three years and living together for four. Her career as a dancer was flourishing, and she was enjoying working and traveling the world. When we married, we did so with one understanding—no children. I had to think deeply about that, as children were always a part of my concept of a family. Eventually though, I decided that I would rather be married to Nanci without children than to someone else with them.

You can imagine my surprise and happiness when, one day, Nanci began talking about having children. Soon we had a healthy baby boy, Patrick. Enjoying our first child so much, we decided that Patrick needed a brother or sister. Nanci and I started down the baby trail again.

Soon Nanci was pregnant again. We were very excited to see the first ultrasound and make a connection with the newest member of our family—another boy. We decided to name him Andrew Joseph. We would call him by his initials, A.J.

Everything was progressing swimmingly, when a precautionary test result came back with some anomalies. The doctors at the clinic wanted to double-check the results with a more conclusive test. They told us not to worry.

It worried us anyway and we immediately began chanting. After having an amniocentesis, when they take a sample of the baby's cells directly from the amniotic fluid, we received conclusive results: A.J. had a chromosome disorder called trisome 18. This condition occurs in the first sixty-four divisions of the cells. The cells from that point do not divide properly and chromosome irregularities continue into every aspect of the baby's development. The doctor told us that this condition was "not compatible with life," and even if the baby made it to term, he would only live a few hours past birth.

We were devastated. Nanci and I started chanting, as is taught in Buddhism, "to change poison into medicine." The issue of "what to do" became increasingly more difficult to discuss. Talking about it led to crying, which led to fighting, which led to not talking about much of anything.

The weight of this decision was proving to be an incredible strain on our marriage. I was surprised by the effect it had on our relationship. As difficult as the news about our son was, equally shocking to me was what was happening in my marriage. From my point of view, Nanci had become a totally different person. She was saying things to me that I had never heard her say before, ever. It was surreal. After seventeen years, I felt like I was married to a stranger. I wondered if I would be able to stay married to her when this chapter closed.

Since I tend to be the kind of person who likes to control

the things around him, I panicked now, suddenly being so out of control. Whatever was happening in my relationship with my wife plagued me almost every minute of every day. That compounded with the dilemma of my unborn son was almost too much for me to bear.

I continued to chant more and more deeply, trying to make some sense out of what was going on. Through all of my sadness and pain, I never felt or chanted with the feeling of being a victim. I just thought, *There must be something I'm not seeing.*

I seemed to be living on two emotional planes. When I thought about my relationship with Nanci or my son A.J., I was overcome with sorrow, unable to hold back the tears. At the same time, I understood that whatever was happening to me was integral to my happiness. When I viewed my circumstances from that perspective, I felt tranquil inside, my tears giving way to a deep sense of appreciation. As I continued to chant in this way, I began to have the profound feeling that it was impossible for this situation to have manifested in my life without having profound significance.

Two thoughts continually plagued me, *What have I missed?* And *How could I have misjudged my wife so completely?*

As I continued to chant for some kind of clarity, I challenged myself to pray for my wife's happiness. I searched my mind for what could possibly be at the crux of her personality U-turn. It was then that I suddenly realized the problem. It was me! I was the problem. In that moment it became abundantly clear that she had never been any different than she had ever been. I just refused to see her for who she was. I saw her only as the person she needed to be for me. I had never truly accepted or appreciated her. The dilemma of our son's life had simply made something more important to her than trying to please me every moment—something I had unknowingly been demanding.

I also realized that the conditions of my expectations, in regard to my definition of a loving wife, and consequently the demands I made of her, were unreasonable and demeaning. How could I have done that to anyone, much less the woman I love?

While the puzzle of my relationship began to take shape, I was now besieged with the horrors of my behavior. As I continued to chant, conversation after conversation, event after event started floating into my mind—all seventeen years worth. The innumerable times I had insisted she say or do something in a certain way. If she didn't, it meant that she didn't understand my needs and was incapable of supporting me. Or worse, it meant that she didn't really love me.

After years of chanting, there is no way I could do something like this! Doesn't Buddhism teach the absolute respect of each individual just as they are? SGI President Ikeda always talks about the impeccable way men should treat women, especially their wives. How could I have so unrelentingly pounded this woman into the mold of who I thought she needed to be?

Then came the lightning bolt. This is what my whole life had been about. This is what I had always done in every single relationship I ever had. Ever since I was a little boy, pleasing people was always my single and only objective. If I didn't fit someone else's mold, I would try to become what I thought they expected me to be. If I thought someone didn't like me or if I thought I had upset virtually anyone in some way, real or imagined, I would suffer endlessly until I could somehow find a way to get back into their good graces. I would change to whatever emotional environment I might find myself in irrespective of the implications it had for me, in order to please someone. I was afraid to be myself, to speak my own mind. Consequently, when I was with anyone of consequence, whose approval I so desperately needed, I usually became an insecure mess. Besides the tremendous amount of energy this behavior required, basing my self-esteem on others' opinions made me terribly unhappy.

These feelings never motivated me to change—until A.J. This would be the purpose of his existence for me. A.J. had appeared to help his stubborn and arrogant father see that there was no way he could be happy if he continued in his present ways. I was overcome with emotion. I understood in the depths of my being why he had come into my life. It became so clear to me that my resistance to this truth about myself was hidden so deeply inside me, that I was incapable of seeing this aspect of my personality in any other way. I wept uncontrollably. It was as if a heavy weight had been lifted from me. And indeed, one had.

My heart overflowed with appreciation. I was astounded and humbled by the power of Buddhism. It validated the promise of the certainty of happiness and freedom that all who practice Nichiren Buddhism will ultimately experience.

As for A.J., we decided not to take him to term. As unbearable as this choice was for us to make, fundamentally, Nanci and I understood and accepted that we were making the right decision. It remains, however, the saddest and most difficult moment of our lives.

As it turns out, this journey was one of relationships for me. The relationship with my son A.J., defining my relationship with my wife, my relationship with my Buddhist practice, ultimately leading to the most fundamental relationship of all—the one with myself.

Today, Nanci and I are still married, and happily so. We did not give up. We went on to have another baby, another boy, Michael. Our family bond is now complete with the children I thought we would never have, the children who have brought us deep and meaningful life lessons and immeasurable joy—our boys, Patrick, Michael and A.J.

Following My Own Footsteps
Aparna P. Khadkikar

*Nothing is at last sacred but the
integrity of your own mind.*
—Ralph Waldo Emerson

I CAME FROM AN INDIAN FAMILY that had a very dynamic and patriotic ancestral lineage. My great-grandfather and grandfather fought against the British rule in India along with Mahatma Gandhi and were ahead of their time in terms of the respect they extended to the women of our family.

I followed in the footsteps of my mother in terms of education, but confidence and self-esteem were alien to me. I was tormented by my lack of beauty, and with this came the baggage of insecurities. Despite a PhD and a prestigious fellowship at the University of Rochester, my lack of confidence was at an all-time low. Somehow all this had translated into a deep longing for a marriage, because I believed that only marriage would make me feel happy and fulfilled.

In addition to these feelings, my attitude toward my research work was not good. I just felt as if nothing worked. I blamed my inadequate performance on an obnoxious boss and racist colleagues. Consequently, I began my fellowship with defeat—and my environment responded. Within six months, my advisor told me my performance did not meet his standards. I was now at the point of losing my job, I had no friends, the excitement of seeing snow had worn off and my prince was showing no signs of appearing to rescue me from this mess. Then I attended my first SGI meeting.

I started chanting everywhere and anywhere—before my experiments, during my experiments, before sleeping, when I was nervous, when I was low, before talking to my advisor, after talking to my advisor—you name it, I chanted.

My research project was the lynchpin on which the entire laboratory's project depended. We were one of the few teams in the world trying to develop a completely new methodology that would revolutionize the field of identifying tumor antigens for cancer vaccines. My boss wanted impossible results. While everyone within and outside my lab had concurred with my fatalist attitude, Buddhism was teaching me to pray to make the impossible possible. I began to work impossible hours, chanting a lot and learning more about Nichiren Buddhism I was practicing by attending regular meetings and learning to recite the morning and evening prayers. I actually began to have an uncompromising prayer.

I delivered the impossible results. Empowered with my success, I developed the capacity to pray for my colleagues to achieve similar results. They did. On the basis of our joint work, my advisor received a grant for two million dollars to start a biotech company. The person who was ready to fire me within months of joining was volunteering my name for seminars and conference presentations, extended my contract for another two years and very happily agreeing to sponsor my green card!

All this elation did not spill over into my personal life. I met suitor after suitor, and I wanted to run away from each within fifteen minutes of meeting them. I was appalled at the quality of men in the arranged-marriage market. And yet it always came down to me not being good enough. I was learning that until I could fall in love with myself, I could never fall for anyone else.

I dug my heels into my Buddhist practice. I was willing to do anything to change my lack of self-love and my destiny. I even overcame my hesitation to tell my parents that I had started to practice Buddhism. I told them during one of my weekly calls home when they remarked that I sounded so much happier and more confident. I continued to chant and my opportunities for change started to arise from the place they had begun—my family.

In March, I received a call from my brother—my mother who had no previous history of illness had become very ill. She had lost her speech, her movement and was unconscious. Ten thousand miles away from her, I felt helpless. I could not rush to her side since I was in the middle of my green card process. With no recourse but to chant, I pulled myself together and prayed for her recovery.

A brain scan would reveal lesions on her brain. For six days as she lay in the intensive care unit, the doctors were baffled. They could not diagnose her illness. One day I would hear cancer, the next day multiple sclerosis. Her symptoms did not clearly fit in with any disease. I prayed for hours every day. My prayers grew uncompromising, "I will not accept my mother in any other condition than she was in before this sickness. I will only accept a full recovery and for her to be stronger and more beautiful than before."

I talked to my father and brothers every day. I sensed their need for my moral and emotional support. I told them about Buddhism and its limitless power and that through the power of prayer our mother would be OK. I faxed them articles and experiences from the Buddhist publications. They were so encouraged that they not only started chanting in earnest, but they began sharing the articles with other patients and their family members on the hospital floor.

For twenty days there was no diagnosis for my mother, however, and because there was no diagnosis, no treatment could begin. Crucial time was being lost.

The fact that I was in Rochester and not in India by my mother's side turned out to be a plus—evidence that prayer can deliver better answers than our best thinking. First, "by accident" I came across a visiting professor who was a specialist in multiple sclerosis. When I described my mother's condition, he immediately knew that it was not MS but ADEM, a disease that was very rare in the tropics, and for my mother's age, but it could be treated and it was not a recurring illness. I had a diagnosis, ten thousand miles away.

After a long recovery process, my mother resumed her job as a professor, and in a break from tradition, the university offered her 75 percent reimbursement of all her medical expenses. Such is the power of Buddhism, the power of strong prayer and the reward of not giving up or giving in.

I was changing the dynamic in my family. Where I had been insecure and suffering from low self-esteem with no confidence, I became a strong person of faith with belief in my life's tremendous potential. Because of it, I was also changing those inherent thoughts that kept me from allowing a relationship into my life. But I wasn't quite there yet.

More study, more prayer and more introspection. After a long chanting session, it dawned on me that marriage or no marriage, I owed it to myself to become truly happy. My strong desire of longing for a man was getting transformed into a desire for awakening to the truth of my own life, awakening my Buddhahood. Once I felt this freedom, a prayer for the happiest marriage came naturally and without any baggage.

Soon, I met my mate. When he pursued me, I surprised myself by not falling all over him. Rather, I told him I needed time to pray and think. In this modern age, he proposed to me over a cell phone. We got married within two months. He is a wonderful human being who respects me and cherishes me and gives me lots of space. He has all the qualities that I wanted in a man but could not have attracted until I did the internal work. We now have two sons.

I have carved my happiness for myself with my faith and my prayers—not through another person, but deep inside of myself.

I was born in India and found the true meaning of life in America. I feel Nichiren Daishonin was talking directly to me when he wrote: "Hsüan-tsang journeyed throughout India in search of the Buddha's teachings for seventeen years. . . . Dengyo remained in T'ang China for only two years, but he traveled three thousand *ri* across the billowing sea to get there. These were all men, ancients, worthies, and sages. Never have I heard of a woman who journeyed a thousand *ri* in search of Buddhism as you did."

Practicing Buddhism has given me tools to bring out the potential within me that I never even knew existed.

CHASING MY HEART

DENVER E. LONG

If the only prayer you ever say in your entire life
is thank you, it would be enough.
—MEISTER ECKHART

WHEN I WAS A CHILD, I spent a lot of time talking to myself. Nothing seemed more natural than for me to ask myself a question and then wait for the answer. And the answers always came. They came from the "voice" inside me. When I wanted to know the truth about something, it never failed.

As I grew older, I confided totally in the wisdom of the voice inside. It always knew my heart's passion and the things I wanted out of life. I wanted to live in very interesting and unique places—which would satisfy the artistic side of me. I wanted to earn college degrees and travel the world. I also wanted to be a college professor and teach. But most importantly, I wanted to find my life's mate, fall in love and live happily ever after.

As the years went by, the voice became fainter and fainter, until I could no longer hear it. It wouldn't be until years later, when I began chanting, that the voice would return. Little did I know that it was my inner wisdom, my higher self, or as the Buddhists say, my Buddha nature and not an invisible childhood friend. That voice would be with me all my life. It would just be my ability to listen that would make the difference.

One week after I received my bachelor's degree in industrial design, I was on a plane headed for Washington, D.C., to begin training as a US Peace Corps volunteer. My assignment was Sierra Leone, West Africa. My home state of Indiana was about to become a distant memory.

My first phase of training would be in Washington D.C., for language and custom classes, then off to the Jamaica School of Agriculture for the next phase.

Because of a passport snafu, I arrived in Jamaica on July 7, four days later than the rest of my group. Consequently, when I got there I was the only person left to register and get a room assignment. Off to the school office I went to start the process.

A pretty young Jamaican girl was there to get me registered. Her name was Joan. With nobody else there to be registered, I got all of Joan's attention. She asked me a few questions. I gave her a few answers and flirted with her a bit. After about ten minutes, I looked at her and announced that she was going to be the girl I would marry. I assured her that she needn't worry. It might take me another ten or fifteen minutes to win her over, or ten or fifteen years. It didn't matter. Eventually, she was going to be my wife. She laughed so hard that we became instant friends. I began sending letters and photos back home to my family telling them about my "Jamaican Doll."

I left Jamaica for the next phase of my training. I was off to the University of the West Indies in the US Virgin Islands, and then on to my two-year assignment at the Union Teacher's College in Bunumbu, Sierra Leone, West Africa.

Eventually, I ended up living in Chicago, jobless and depressed from a recent breakup with my girlfriend. Then a friend introduced me to Nichiren Buddhism. At first I fought with him and argued until we finally made a deal. He told me to chant for whatever I wanted. What I wanted was a three-story graystone mansion located in the old historic district where Chicago's early millionaires used to live. The deal was that I would chant an hour a day and do the morning and evening prayers every day for thirty days. If I didn't have the mansion by then, he agreed never to mention Buddhism or chanting to me again. He explained that when you start to chant, you elevate your attitude, or life-condition, and the negativity in your life begins to surface. It surfaces to purify your life and environment.

I didn't believe a word of it, but I started chanting every day mainly to prove him wrong. I was told that the key to success was consistency—to keep chanting no matter what.

I began sitting on the steps of an empty mansion that I wanted, chanting and practicing my evening prayers. I would do that every evening as the sun went down. I would then chant for hours. I started to attract a very odd group of onlookers. I was on a quiet, isolated street and I wondered where they came from. They were odd, standing at the bottom of the stairs looking up at me, mumbling, walking in circles and generally amusing themselves. Who were these strange people? Was this a representation of what I had inside of me? As it turned out, they were just a group of patients from the local mental hospital. They had been intrigued by the sound of the chanting. Some of them even tried to chant with me. I figured that they were either a representation of my own lunacy for trying this experiment, or they were just more pure in spirit then the rest of us and they were attracted to the spiritual aspect of my chanting. In either case, I kept chanting.

Through an amazing series of events, thirty days later I moved into that mansion. The first thing that I moved in was my Buddhist altar.

After that, true to my friend's words, things from deep inside my life began to surface. Most of it had to do with relationships. I received word that my best friend in Indiana had died. My father and I attended the wake and stood at his casket mourning the loss of our dear friend. A few weeks later, I was standing in that very same spot, at the very same funeral home, at the casket of my father who had died suddenly. Then my aunt and two more of my friends died. I was profoundly confused and depressed, but through it all I continued to chant.

Then one evening, as I chanted Nam-myoho-renge-kyo, I heard the voice again. It was like a childhood friend come back. I was profoundly touched. Suddenly, Joan came to mind. I began chanting for Joan, the young lady I had met in Jamaica, to come back into my life. I didn't know if she was still in Jamaica, or if she was even still alive. I just began chanting with all my heart, even though I had not seen or heard from her since I left Jamaica years before.

For about two weeks I had been chanting for her when one evening, as I was doing my evening prayers, the phone rang and to my absolute, utter amazement, it was Joan!

When I asked her how she found me and why she was calling, she told me that she had been thinking about me for the last couple of weeks. She was now living in New York and was about to visit a cousin who lived in Evanston, a suburb close to Chicago. Thinking about how close Indiana was to where she was going, she decided to call directory assistance to try and find me. After about two calls, she got my mother. My mother immediately knew who she was from all the letters and photos I had sent back home when I was in Jamaica.

My Buddhist practice led me to an appreciation of all of the relationships that I had in my life. I learned how to value and cherish people and how not to take them for granted. In having more respect and appreciation for the precious relationships I did have, Joan came back into my life. And on July 7, exactly sixteen years after we met that day in her office, I married my sweet Jamaican doll.

THE HONEYMOON

CARLOS GASCON

Buddhism teaches that, when the
Buddha nature manifests itself from within,
it will receive protection from without.
—NICHIREN DAISHONIN

MY STORY BEGINS IN SPRING 2004 when someone told me about chanting Nam-myoho-renge-kyo. These were strange words to me, words I didn't pay much attention to, at first.

My life, at that moment in time, was a little chaotic. Things weren't going badly for me, but they could have been better; it seemed like I was stuck in a rut. My work didn't seem to be getting off the ground, and my girlfriend, Marisa, was in a similar situation. Our lives just weren't in gear. Everything moved forward, but slowly, like a machine forced to work, a machine in need of a good oiling. Our lives needed something that would enable the pieces to work together with more harmony.

Against all my principles I decided to try chanting these words that had been given to me with such enthusiasm. Without much conviction, and a bit of disdain, I attended a discussion meeting in order to understand why on earth I was doing this. I wasn't very aware of what had begun, but in those words I did find meaning.

Meanwhile, "coincidentally" there were some sudden

unexpected changes for the better in my girlfriend's job, and she began to chant, too. We began thinking more seriously about Nichiren Buddhism, and we looked into receiving the Gohonzon for our home so that we could chant there. I considered it an honor to receive one. For me, it would become an outward symbol of our commitment to this ancient and beautiful philosophy. Once this commitment was made, our lives began to change radically. So many amazing things began to happen that it is difficult to even relate them all. Some of them were deep internal and significant changes. I, myself, am still in the process of understanding them and the impact that they are making in my life.

Marisa and I had been together for fourteen years, and we realized it was time to define our relationship and make a commitment to one another. We decided to get married. We began our wedding preparations and planned on celebrating this happy occasion with our closest family and friends. We decided to treat ourselves to a fantastic holiday and honeymoon. Plans were under way—we started making hotel reservations, buying plane tickets and mapping out our amazing honeymoon. Then, with an excited new commitment, we bought two rings. Every day we recited our morning and evening prayers, always taking time to especially chant about our plans and our trip. The wedding would take place on Saturday, December 11, 2004.

I am an actor by profession, and the day before our wedding I "coincidentally" got a call for an audition. Of all times! But it was for an important part in a new television series, and it would begin filming immediately! I told them I was getting married the next day and we were leaving for our honeymoon on the following Monday.

At the audition, I told them that if they wanted me for the series they would have to decide very quickly. They congratulated me on my upcoming wedding and indicated that the audition had gone well. When I left the audition, something told me I wouldn't be going on my honeymoon.

Marisa and I decided to proceed with our plans anyway. I remember packing the suitcases having no idea what would happen, or even if we would need them at all. Our plane was leaving at two in the afternoon and we were planning to be on it as if nothing had happened. At eleven that morning, the casting director called me at home to tell me he was in a meeting with the executives of the television station; they were deciding on the cast, but at that moment, he still couldn't give me a concrete answer.

Nervously, we left for the airport, my new wife didn't know if she was coming or going. I knew intuitively that I shouldn't complain or be worried about the situation. I would instead trust the hours of prayers that had gone into our plans.

The trip to the airport was marvelous. I felt immersed in an aura of well-being, completely confident that the very best thing for my life was going to happen. How could I lose either way? On one hand, if we didn't take our trip it meant that I got the job—an important job that would make a difference in my career. It would be the culmination of all the work I'd done for so many years as an actor. On the other hand, I knew that if we did get on that plane, we would have an unforgettable honeymoon.

We arrived at the airport and while we were standing in line to check in, I received a call that I'll remember forever.

"Where are you? Don't get on the plane. You've got the part!"

Between kisses, tears and a dizzy feeling of joy, we left the airport and returned home. The next day I started my new job—a wonderful television role.

Of course, we were a bit sad to have abandoned our honeymoon after making all the exciting plans and anticipating a holiday that would commemorate our commitment to each other. We were looking forward to that trip and the lifetime of memories it would have given us. But, as it turns out, our prayers served us well. Not only did I get the job of a lifetime but also, even though we didn't know it at the time, we were being protected.

On the day that we had planned on luxuriating on a beautiful beach in Phuket, Thailand, a tsunami occurred in the Indian Ocean taking thousands of lives in one gigantic wave. We were not there. We were not meant to be.

Falling in Love

Virginia Straus Benson

Ideal love is fostered only between two sincere,
mature and independent people. It is essential, therefore,
that you make polishing yourself a priority and
do not get carried away by romance.

—Daisaku Ikeda

WHEN I BEGAN TO PRACTICE Nichiren Buddhism many years ago, I was told that I could accomplish all my dreams, and the idea thrilled me. I was thirty-five then, and most of my dreams already had come crashing down. One closest to my heart was the dream that I would find my soul mate and live happily ever after. *Cinderella* was my favorite fairy tale when I was young. I even named my dog Cinderella.

So far, however, my Prince Charmings had been anything but. I had sleepwalked into a miserable marriage in my twenties that was more Greek tragedy than fairy tale. Just like in *Pygmalion*, my husband was sure I would be better as someone else. Since my sense of self-identity was shaky anyway, I cooperated. I twisted myself every which way, but I was never the person he wanted.

After my divorce and several other heartbreaks, I realized that I was attracted to men who disrespected and dominated me. I developed a fear of being controlled by a man, and so I deliberately steered away from men I was attracted to.

When I studied Nichiren Buddhism and learned about the oneness of self and environment, it put my unhappy love life in perspective. I had been choosing the reflection of my self-doubt and low self-esteem. Prince Charming might change his mask, but the inner drama remained the same.

The Gohonzon, the object of devotion in Nichiren Buddhism, fascinated me. As I understood it, Nichiren Daishonin had inscribed a scroll that could reflect back to me the inner condition of human enlightenment buried within me. How profound and deeply reassuring! I chanted with all my heart for true confidence based on the belief in my potential for the Buddha's life-state.

I assumed I would naturally meet a man who would respect me for the Buddha I really am. I didn't realize how long it would take for me, the woman with the shaky self-identity, to develop my true self.

For more than twenty years, I practiced faithfully and experienced huge transformations in every area except my love life. For example, in my career, I went from a burned-out policy wonk to the founding director of two think tanks, the latest being a dream job as head of the Boston Research Center for the 21st Century, a peace institute that SGI President Ikeda established.

Also, after struggling for most of my life with serious mood swings, I attained emotional stability. Through chanting more whenever I was down in the dumps, studying Buddhism and doing SGI-USA activities surrounded by upbeat Buddhists, I conquered this stubborn tendency.

But dating? That was another story.

Where had all the men gone? It was a desert. Each new possibility turned out to be a mirage. In Nichiren Buddhism, we learn that no prayer goes unanswered, so where was the answer to mine?

Many wonderful fellow Buddhists encouraged me along the way. I had thought, *I'll move to a place where I can find more single men.* Instead, my leader encouraged me, "Strengthen the orbit of your faith, and the right one will come to you." I understood his words to mean that I should sink my roots and strengthen my practice right where I was. A noble life, shining with purpose, would attract its like.

After years of Buddhist practice, I became discouraged. Maybe I should have been chasing after men instead of doing Buddhist activities. Had I been wasting my time? I met with a women's leader in Japan and poured out my heart. Her answer was, "You may never marry." I cried and cried. No one had ever said that to me. But, she continued, "If you carry out your mission as a bodhisattva, a practicing Buddhist working for peace, you'll be completely fulfilled by the end of your life, whether you're married or not." She told me to chant until I felt in my gut that this was true.

It took me about three months. Finally, I understood that true victory was not marriage. It was an undeniable sense of fulfillment, and it would be mine if I lived as a bodhisattva. I stopped having bouts of loneliness.

But still, I wanted a partner. I felt like the odd woman out; I had a nagging sense that something might be wrong with me because I was in my fifties and no man had chosen me. And anyway, most married people were no happier than single people. Gradually, I understood that I was fine just as I was. His words helped me break the grip of a patriarchal stereotype about "old maids."

Then my beloved mother died, and through chanting, I transformed my troubled relationship with my father and found the compassion to inspire him to live on without her. I saw the goodness in my father instead of stereotyping him as just another male dominator. During this process, I felt I changed my negative karma with men.

Around this time, I spoke with an SGI-USA leader. She empathized with my desire for a partner and said, "Ginny, I think you'll meet him by serendipity." To me, this meant that my happiness would unfold naturally. Her compassion moved me, and I realized that my mission as a bodhisattva was profound and embraced my dream for a satisfying intimate relationship.

With these two shifts—believing in my father's Buddha potential (and by extension, the potential of men) and realizing the uniquely personal nature of my mission—I continued to chant about a relationship. I developed a solid sense of self based on faith and, as a result, all my relationships reflected greater depth and intimacy.

In April 2004, I boarded an airplane bound for California. Sitting in my seat, thinking it was his, was my soul mate, Don. We talked and laughed and confided in each other all the way to Los Angeles, his home.

Everything he loves about me I built through my Buddhist practice. He thinks I have an inner radiance. (I know this

comes from years of chanting Nam-myoho-renge-kyo.)
He's interested in my work at the peace center and respects
my devotion to it. He loves the fact that I have so many
close friends and connections. He appreciates Buddhism
and the warmth of our Buddhist community.

When I flew to Minneapolis to meet Don's family, I had
to change planes in Chicago. Don unexpectedly boarded
my flight. Smiling, he said, "This time, *you* are in the wrong
seat." Acting just like Prince Charming, he led me to a
reserved seat and proposed. Don moved to Boston on
Valentine's Day. We had a June wedding.

Recently, Don met my friend in California who encouraged me and told her, "I'm Mr. Serendipity." He said the
look on her face of pure joy for our victory convinced him
of the altruistic bonds forged by women in our Buddhist
community.

Reflecting on my inner journey to find Mr. Serendipity, I
am moved by the profound workings of Buddhist prayer.
As President Ikeda has said: "There are many elements
involved in a prayer being answered, but the important
thing is to keep praying until it is. By continuing to pray,
you can reflect on yourself with unflinching honesty and
begin to move your life in a positive direction on the path
of earnest, steady effort. Even if your prayer doesn't produce concrete results immediately, your continual prayer
will at some time manifest itself in a form greater than you
had ever hoped."

My High School Sweetheart

Joyce Truitt

The Buddha promised in the Lotus Sutra that, for women, the sutra will serve as a lantern in the darkness, as a ship when they cross the sea, and as a protector when they travel through dangerous places.
—Nichiren Daishonin

This is my story. I am seventy-five years old.

My son, Steven, introduced me to Nichiren Buddhism in Texas. Soon after that he became very ill, suffering from Crohn's disease, which led to two life-saving surgeries.

During this time, members encouraged me to chant. They told me there is no prayer stronger then the prayer of a mother for her child. At his hospital bedside, I learned to recite the Buddhist daily prayers. Today he is the picture of health, and he's had no recurrences.

In less than a year after that, my husband had a heart attack. Six months later he was diagnosed with pancreatic cancer. He chose not to have treatment. He developed dementia and died within three months. It was the death of an alcoholic. I felt ravaged.

Again, Buddhist friends were at my side helping me through. The advice that sustained me was to "Imagine you are having a bad dream and know that you will wake up and it will soon be over."

For the next five years, I became very active in my Buddhist group. The encouragement and guidance provided were the fundamentals I needed. Many years earlier, as my children grew and needed less attention, I became a patient volunteer for our local hospice. Never did I dream that I would become the recipient of these same services when my husband fell ill. I deeply appreciate their role in managing every aspect of dying and grief.

Having lost a mate, I am much more understanding as a volunteer. Some of my most rewarding experiences in life have been befriending, listening and encouraging a dying patient in their last days. I chanted with and for every one of these patients. I have recently added bereavement support to my training, allowing me to follow through with my grieving families.

I had been a widow for five years, and on New Year's Day, I made my resolutions like everybody else. The most significant one I made was to fill the void in my life left by my husband's death. I wanted a male companion. The only stipulations were that he be taller than me, and that he be my very best friend. I resolved, and then I chanted.

Valentine's Day came and my heart ached with loneliness. That night I dreamed of my high school sweetheart. In the dream he was curled up in a fetal position, very, very sad.

The next morning, a friend of mine—who just happens to live in the same town as my high school sweetheart—called me. I told her about my dream. She looked him up and gave me his address and his phone number. I finally mustered up the courage to ask my friend if she would call him to see if he was OK. She agreed.

The hours dragged. She returned my call late in the evening. She had gotten in touch with him. They had a nice visit and she was ready to hang up when he said, "She knows, doesn't she, that my wife died in October?"

I was so excited I shook all over. Of course, I had to phone him and I did. It seemed we talked for hours about everything under the sun.

That conversation has yet to end. We have been together for nine years and I am truly, truly happy. We spend the summers at his cottage in the north woods and a month in the winter in Texas, so I can be near my sons.

I am so grateful for having found Nichiren Buddhism. My experiences have given me confidence to engage in meaningful dialogues, to inspire and to motivate others and to live every moment of my life to the fullest with my high school sweetheart, who is taller than me, and who is my best friend.

7

aging and death

*Buddhism views the idea that our lives end with death
as a serious delusion. It sees everything in the universe,
everything that happens, as part of a vast living web of
interconnection. The vibrant energy we call life, which
flows throughout the universe has no beginning and no
end. Life is a continuous, dynamic process of change.
Why then should human life be the one exception?
Why should our existence be an arbitrary, one-shot deal,
disconnected from the universal rhythms of life?*
—DAISAKU IKEDA

T HE INCORPORATION OF Nichiren Buddhism into
peoples' lives—as the stories in this book reveal—
changes the course that they might have followed.
Consequently, when a person begins aging and faces death,
the experience becomes entirely different than it could
have been.

255

From a Buddhist perspective, our ability to pass successfully through our last years and the dying process depends
on our steady efforts during life to accumulate good causes,
to contribute to the happiness of others and to strengthen
the foundation of goodness and humanity in the depths of
our lives. Having thus been a victor in life, we can win in
death as well.

We practice Buddhism to live happily, to age happily and
to die happily. Buddhism guarantees that those who practice sincerely will see aging as a vibrant "third stage" of life
and approach death in a state of supreme fulfillment.

Victory over death. Sounds preposterous at first. We all
must die eventually. No one can avoid it. Yet, the stories
that follow clearly demonstrate that aging and death can be
positive, life affirming and even joyful.

Armed with a sound philosophy, Nichiren Buddhists
tend to face growing old as a natural and noble state, and
face terminal illness or the recent passing of a loved one
with a sense of optimism, appreciation and, indeed, victory
over the usual sufferings associated with death.

Aging and death come to everyone. What is important is
whether the experience is a positive one. Since death is natural, Nichiren Buddhism believes there is no reason that it
need be negative. This is possible for one who embraces the
Buddhist perspective on life and death.

My Grandfather
Marc Sachnoff

To lead a life in which we are inspired and can inspire others, our hearts have to be alive; they have to be filled with passion and enthusiasm.
—Daisaku Ikeda

GROWING UP, I WAS FORTUNATE to have my grandparents living near us. I spent many fun hours playing penny poker with them and talking about business, politics and their travels around the world. My grandmother was a great cook as well as an artist and a sculptor. My grandfather was the patriarch of the family. I never saw him ever get sick or even take an aspirin. More than six feet tall, with a commanding voice, he was the kind of strong figure who held the family together through thick and thin.

So you can imagine my shock when I received a phone call that Grandpa had had a heart attack while visiting my cousins in Seattle. The family was in shock and Grandpa was in a coma.

I had been chanting a few years, but in that brief time I had been able to introduce my grandmother to chanting. Although she was already in her eighties when she started, she took to chanting very naturally. When she called I encouraged her to chant for Grandpa's complete recovery—total success. But inside I was worried. As the days progressed, Grandpa's state did not change. And as I had been told, the longer someone stays in the intensive care unit of a hospital the less likely it is that they'll ever recover.

I kept encouraging my grandmother and continued chanting lots. I knew that I had to fly to Seattle and take the strength I'd gained through my Buddhist practice and apply it to the family crisis in person. I'd just started a new job, and my boss was willing to let me take a few days off, so I sold the Oriental rug off my living room floor, bought a ticket and prepared to leave to join my mother, uncles, aunts and cousins who had already converged on the hospital. But before I left, I realized that I needed to get some advice from a trusted Buddhist friend. The person I sought out had always encouraged me, even if he was often blunt. This time was no different. He told me that if I were planning to help the situation, I would have to take 100 percent responsibility for my grandfather's life, using this opportunity to try to repay my debt of gratitude to him. If I was unwilling to do this, I shouldn't even bother flying up there, as I'd only make things worse.

On the bumpy flight from Los Angeles to Seattle, I mulled over his words. I was determined to help, but how? When I arrived, I could see that things had taken a turn for the worse. My grandfather, the strong man of the family, was in a vegetative coma, thrashing around in a hospital bed that was too small for him, tethered in a thicket of wires, tubes and straps. My relatives were also a mess as none of them had ever thought they would see Grandpa in this condition—it shook and saddened them deeply. Some were even preparing for his death as if it was a foregone conclusion.

I, however, had determined to get to work. After a brief

family meeting, I told my grandmother that my plan was to chant—chant for wisdom, chant to pierce Grandpa's life and chant for the best possible care. My grandmother joined me, but because of the stress of the situation and her age, she tired after a while and I encouraged her to rest. I told her I would continue. I would take 100 percent responsibility. The rest of the family remained skeptical and some were downright hostile about "that Buddhist stuff." As I chanted to my comatose grandfather, I hardly noticed what was going on around me. But first I was paid a visit by a nun. I thanked her for her concern but told her that I had the situation in hand. After a few more hours of chanting by the bedside, I was visited by a rabbi. I thanked him as well but told him that I was a Buddhist and had my own way of working through this challenge. But still I wasn't sure what to do beyond chanting furiously.

On the second day, after hours more of chanting, it began to sink into my life. I had to repay my debt of gratitude—all the years of love and support, gifts and ball games, dinner and travel. But more than that, he was a great role model of an honorable man, my mother's father, without whom I would not have shown up on the planet. I owed him more than I realized and I suddenly determined that I would pay it back, even if just a little, right here, right now.

I looked at the sad figure before me. A drugged, disheveled man in his mid-eighties, eyes staring emptily, in an ill-fitting gown on an ill-fitting bed, his breathing forced by a large respirator machine. This had to change.

I tried to contact him through my chanting as if I was

sending a light beam into his life. Would he respond to me? I chanted as if to tell him that if he could hear or feel me that he should move his right arm. No response. Move his left arm. No response. For a moment I became disheartened. Then I remembered how a Buddhist leader had once responded to a hospitalized, terminally ill member. He bounded into the dark room, grabbed her hand and called the name of the member loudly. I'll never forget the face of this woman—I mean, she was dying. I thought she was almost gone, but at the sound of his voice or should I say the presence of his life-condition, she responded. She opened her eyes and smiled. I knew if I could bring out that kind of life-condition, I would have a chance at really helping my grandfather in his darkest moment.

Then it came to me. The man was a fighter all his life— football champ, baseball star—he always gave 100 percent given the chance. I called in my grandmother. We have to tell the doctors to take Grandpa off all the medications. We need to see if he's still "there." She was skeptical, but I was on fire. She knew that I was onto something and her own wisdom told her to trust this radical idea.

The doctor was more than skeptical. He thought we could be endangering his life. "What life?" I responded. He resisted. I told him and Grandma that I would take total responsibility. Then she stood up and instructed the doctor to do as I said.

As we chanted by his side, within minutes the thrashing stopped. Then I called to him in a loud voice, "Grandpa, if you can hear me nod your head." His head moved up and down weakly. "Are you in pain?" I shouted. He nodded side to side. "Are you ready to fight?" He nodded yes. I turned to the doctor, "Take out the respirator, now!" He was still a bit stunned but he did as asked. Out came the white plastic snake that forced air into my grandfather's paralyzed lungs. As my grandmother and I chanted through our tears, he labored to breathe. He went for fifteen minutes and then his heart rate went up. Back in went the respirator. But down went all the medications. We needed Grandpa fully present for round two. Now all of us, Grandma, the doctor and the family were ready to fight.

The next day he made it to twenty minutes. We were on the way. My boss called. I was needed back on the job or there might be no job. I had to leave. But I knew that I had set in motion a plan whose success I was certain of. On the following day, he slipped back to only fifteen minutes, but on the fourth day the respirator came out for good. Within two days he was moved to a recovery room and within a week he was on a plane back home to Chicago for a triple bypass operation.

He recovered completely, though he lost a bit of his old fire. When I next saw him for the family holiday gathering, he pulled me aside. "I don't know what you did back there, but whatever it was, I want to thank you." I gave him a hug and told him that it was just my way of thanking him for all his love and support over the years.

Though my grandmother and I remained the only consistent Buddhists in the family (and she continued up until her death at ninety-two), I can tell you no one in the family gave me any guff about "that Buddhism stuff" ever again.

TOO MUCH

ZAN GAUDIOSO

You can't cross the sea merely by standing
and staring at the water.
—RABINDRANATH TAGORE

S HE CAME INTO MY LIFE before I was even aware that I was alive. She was my great aunt and I adored her. I was barely two years old and my father had just died, leaving behind my mother and three young children. My mother's grief was so consuming that she was hardly able to go through the motions of life. Her aunt and uncle came from New York to be by her side and ended up moving to California. The very first time they walked into our house I was sound asleep on the living room floor. My aunt walked over to where I was sleeping, looked down at me and said, "She is absolutely too much!" From then on, I would always be known to her as "Too Much." She would be known to me as the only light that wandered into my life, our lives, at a very dark time. She was more than a mother to me; she was my friend, my confidante and my rock. That's why, many years later, when she learned that she had cancer, my world would fall apart.

I had just been introduced to Nichiren Buddhism and immediately started chanting for her. I was sure that I would be able to save her with my sincere prayers. I was certain that I could put into motion circumstances that

262

would incite nothing short of a full recovery. I had heard miraculous stories of other Buddhists who had not only survived their cancer but who had received such clean bills of health that cancer couldn't even be found in their bodies. This had to be the outcome for my aunt. I couldn't conceive of my life without her.

She had practically adopted me. She had two boys of her own, so having a little girl to fawn over was her delight. She and my uncle had moved into this big, beautiful, sprawling house. They even had a two-story barn that would become a playground for my rich fantasy life. My friends and I would play in there for hours. I would stay with my aunt and uncle on weekends and for much of the time in the summer. I would sleep in one of her son's oversized T-shirts and snuggle close to her, drink hot chocolate and talk to her about anything and everything. She provided me with a childhood that would have otherwise been ripped away by my father's sudden death at thirty-six and my mother's inability to cope with her grief. My aunt was such a gift to me then and throughout my life. I simply could not recon-cile myself to her dying.

I had always found such solace in chanting. Somehow it would disconnect the chatter in my head so that I could realign myself with my inner wisdom—that objective per-spective that could offer answers where before there had only been confusion. But in those days I was feeling such despair, I found it hard to chant. The counsel I received was, "No matter what, just keep chanting."

It was also a time in my life that I was facing a career

change and my first really serious love. While I drove my aunt to her radiation treatments every day, I would talk to her about my life, my work and my spirituality. I thought I could help her and bring her some encouragement while she was going through this difficult time; but in fact, I felt lost. I was having a terrible time committing to work, to a relationship, to my life.

All these wonderful things I had wanted, that I had chanted for, sat poised and ready to come into my life. There was only one problem; I was keeping them out. My fear of abandonment and loss were keeping me from committing to my own life and I didn't even know it. And here I was on the verge of losing someone very important to me, again.

In the weeks that followed, as I would drive my aunt to her radiation treatments and sit with her in hospital rooms, she would become the one to support me and teach me how to embrace life. She became my angel—my ambassador for the necessary changes I would have to make in my thinking if I were going to change my life.

One day I was sitting with her in her hospital room and she took my hand and said, "You know, the real loss in life comes when you become too scared to take the opportunities that come your way. We get scared that we're going to lose something that we don't even have! And the irony is that we'll never get it if we don't take the chance. Your father didn't die to leave you with nothing."

At that moment I had a profound realization. All this time I had been feeling sorry for myself because of the losses that

I had suffered. I had perceived my life as being worse off because of them. *If I only had had a father I would have had this option or that opportunity.* In truth, my life would not have been better or worse, it would have just been different. My circumstances had led me down another path—I had always perceived it as the lesser one. These thoughts kept me scared, constricted and unable to commit for fear of being abandoned. My judgment of my situation and my stance as a victim began to melt with that realization.

In the coming weeks I realized that my aunt was going to die. The way I chanted for the situation was different; the way I chanted for my life was different. I was different. I became more willing to risk and I became more confident as a result. A string had been pulled through the fabric of my life and it was creating a beautiful pattern for me, a pattern, which included the lives of my father and my aunt, and the richness that their contributions had made, not the holes that I thought had been created from their absence.

I also chanted that my aunt's death would be easy and painless, that when she died she might experience some of the joy that she had given to others. She died in her son's home, surrounded by family. Her last words to me were, "I love you, Too Much." When she closed her eyes for the last time, she was smiling.

Several months after she died, I had a new career and a wonderful new love in my life. I had let go of a fear of abandonment that was paralyzing me. I had let go of feeling like a victim, which had, in the past, only delivered more circumstances that would allow me to feel sorry for myself. I never questioned my thoughts that were based on fear. They just became habitual thought patterns, which impacted the circumstances I would attract in my life. I never questioned them before, until I started chanting. My prayers for my aunt's recovery delivered circumstances that broke the chain of my own unhappiness. My aunt's death left me feeling more loved, not more abandoned.

I continued to chant for her happiness, and from time to time I could feel her presence. In fact, one day, the wonderful man in my life came up behind me, gave me a hug and said, "Has anyone ever told you that you're simply too much?" I smiled knowing that he was delivering a message, a reminder that she was still with me. I remember thinking to myself, "You bet I have, and because of it, my life will never, ever be the same."

BATTLING FEAR

JUDY MINOR-JACKSON

Memories of our lives, of our works and our deeds
will continue in others.
—ROSA PARKS

I HAVE BATTLED FEAR ALL MY LIFE—that voice that tells me I'm not good enough, not smart enough, not capable enough.

I was twelve when my mother died, and I grew up with a sense of abandonment and fear of death.

When I was in my twenties, my best friend, Isatou, introduced me to Nichiren Buddhism. She also introduced me to the man I would eventually marry. After fifteen years of marriage, I was looking forward to the rest of my life with my husband. He was diagnosed with cancer, however, and died six weeks later. During this very dark time, Isatou and my Buddhist practice helped me find meaning in my life.

I had been working as an auditor for the city of Chicago for twenty years. It was also my twentieth year of practicing Buddhism. It was time for a change.

I chanted to find a better job where I could make a difference. Soon after, I landed a job as a project manager in another division of the city agency I worked for. The job consisted of redeveloping the Engelwood community on the city's southwest side. There was one obstacle: I had no prior experience in land-use planning or community and economic development. I was given a three hundred million dollar budget and immediately became overwhelmed with the responsibility. I chanted and sought advice from a friend in faith. "You can and must make a difference," I was told.

The same month I got the job, my dear friend Isatou was diagnosed with cancer. This was devastating news. We decided to chant more.

Three months later, I received a certificate of recognition for my demonstration of growth within the department and for having sought ways to make a contribution at work. But many of my fears began to surface. Isatou's illness frightened us both; at work, I felt like I did not fit in. I thought that by volunteering for an upcoming political campaign, I could prove something.

What a mistake! It did not help at all. In fact, it caused more problems at work. I was confused and sought advice again. This time, I was encouraged to "focus on making a tremendous difference on your job" rather than in a political campaign. I chanted to make a difference.

I realized later that I should have trusted myself and the power of my faith first. I wanted to make a difference in the community and show validity of Buddhism, which starts with my practice and with changing myself—becoming stronger and wiser.

In April, Isatou had surgery to remove a cancerous tumor. The surgery was successful, but her recovery was slow. Little by little, she regained her strength and went back to work. It was difficult to spend much time with her because I was working ten-hour days and going to graduate school. But I was inspired by her determination and decided to chant with her every morning. She encouraged me by her example—she never gave up.

As I focused on making a difference at work and on deepening my self-confidence, my redevelopment project took off. I briefed Chicago Mayor Richard Daley on the progress, and he informed me that he would make a formal announcement within two weeks about the city's efforts to revitalize Engelwood.

The next day, the doctor informed Isatou that the cancer had returned. We were devastated. I had to find some way to encourage her and not lose hope.

Preparing for the mayor's public announcement and taking care of my best friend, I got up at four each morning to chant two hours before leaving for work. These were very challenging weeks.

In October, Mayor Daley made the formal announcement and acknowledged my hard work to the press. At the press conference, I was exhausted, but I had no fear. The mayor was impressed with my interview, and the press conference was a total success.

After the announcement of the city's efforts to revitalize Engelwood, the project began to get national as well as international attention. I was shocked and delighted. I was soon called to the mayor's office again. This time I was told to prepare to brief President Bill Clinton, who wanted to tour and bring investments into the Engelwood community. I could not believe it—the president coming to Engelwood, a community that no one had paid much attention to in thirty years.

During this period, Isatou became weaker. She could barely walk or talk. I felt the pain of losing my husband all over again.

"I can't take this," I told her.

"You have to," she said. "You have to fight for both of us and not be defeated." She told me to show President Clinton the greatness of Buddhism with my life.

The night before the president arrived, Isatou's condition worsened and we were up all night. The morning of the president's visit, I was terribly sick; you name it, I had it. As the president arrived, helicopters were in the air, people lined up as though for a parade and secret service agents patted me down.

The meeting with President Clinton was a total success. I conveyed everything I understood about the importance of this project, and he committed funds to help revitalize Engelwood. I raced home to tell Isatou and we cried tears of joy together.

National investors contacted me after his visit. I had made a choice to ground my life and advance my career based on faith rather than focus on political circles, and I was finally seeing the result I had wanted.

Isatou's illness progressed until she was bedridden. It was a daily challenge to maintain a fighting spirit as I watched her deteriorate.

Meanwhile, at work, managing three hundred million dollars was not an easy task. My situation was made more difficult when I was not considered for a pay raise. At first I was upset and blamed everyone else. Then I remembered that faith is the basis of my life, and I took responsibility to change my circumstances. I stopped blaming others and did my best at work. A new upper management team came in and immediately promoted me. Faith first, I realized once again.

Isatou died on January 16. My pain was indescribable. Isatou, however, had never given up and neither could I. The next month, I spoke with another friend in faith and was reminded that Isatou did not die before her time and that I also have a mission to fulfill. In other words, focus on the value of life, not on death. This helped me face my fear of death.

I found I could understand the suffering of others in a way I had never experienced before. I had challenged my fears and doubts during Isatou's illness and used my suffering to strengthen bonds with my family and develop a stronger self-identity. Anything is possible, I learned, when we believe and never give up.

I also realized I was no longer overwhelmed by a job for which I had not been prepared. I felt confidence where I had once felt fear.

Now I am a deputy commissioner responsible for the entire South Region of the city of Chicago, the largest region in our city. I manage a large staff and am responsible for the redevelopment of this region.

Watching my good friend face her fears and live more fully because of her trust and faith in Buddhism and watching her die more peacefully because of that faith has taught me to face my own fears. By doing so, through my faith, through chanting, I not only have more joy, I am passing on the legacy and life work of my friend, Isatou.

Rumors of My Death
Darrell Griffin

*To pray, ponder and move for the sake of people's
happiness is to awaken real sincerity.*
—Daisaku Ikeda

WHEN I ATTENDED THE UNIVERSITY of Colorado
in Boulder, my roommate came home one night and
in giant letters wrote on the dorm room wall, the phrase
Nam-myoho-renge-kyo. He said that the meeting he had
just attended inspired him to recite this phrase for whatever he wanted, and that his desire would be fulfilled. He then
informed me that he would chant for a bag of great marijuana. I humored him and chalked it up to just another
"whacko Boulder happening."

I decided to check out for myself these meetings my
roommate was going to.

The meeting was held in an abandoned fraternity house.
Several people were chanting for what seemed like an eternity. When they finished chanting, they sang a few songs
and told me about their experiences with this philosophy. I
remember one person's story in particular. She had been
readying herself to enter a convent to begin training as a
nun. Other members promised that if she was not satisfied
with the benefits received from practicing Nichiren
Buddhism after ninety days, they would all quit and follow
her. Just to prove them wrong she chanted for something

ridiculous like getting red socks sent to her in the mail. A few days later, to her surprise, enclosed in a "care package" from her mother in California were red socks. She was so ecstatically happy about those red socks. I remember at the time thinking, *That's the stupidest thing I ever heard!* But my roommate got his big bag of marijuana—his wish was fulfilled.

A year later, I was standing at a gas station when a car drove up and one of the girls in the car invited me to a meeting and told me a little about it. I told her that I'd gone a year ago and remembered something about red socks. Another girl in the car excitedly shouted, "That was me!" She looked noticeably happier than the last time I had seen her. Since the meeting was less than a block away, I decided to go.

I was impressed by all of the different kinds of people who were there. There were hippies in jeans, people in business suits, people in casual attire and people in cowboy outfits. At the time I hated cowboys, but for some reason I was drawn to this one guy. He said something that has stayed with me to this day: "Chant Nam-myoho-renge-kyo and you can be what you want to be, go where you want to go and do what you want to do." Over time, the constant encouragement I got from this man gave me the guts to continue to practice Nichiren Buddhism. His wife also said something that evening that has had a profound effect on me: "Buddhism is like music. With correct practice, someday all you will have to do is think something, and it will happen." I started practicing the next day.

Years later, I had a major health event that resulted in me being pronounced dead. Since I don't remember anything from when I was "dead," the following account of what happened to me is by my friend:

On Sunday, March 28, 2004, at around five in the afternoon, Darrell was pulling carpet out of a closet for a friend. By half past five, he was in the intensive care unit at the Colorado University Medical Center. When I arrived at the hospital, Darrell was in a coma. The staff told me that he had stopped breathing for about twenty minutes and for me not to be too hopeful. They had him on life support. They told me that he was essentially dead. The only thing keeping him alive was the machine he was hooked up to. He had numerous tubes in him, but there was no activity on the monitors. The hospital has a procedure of keeping patients in Darrell's circumstance on life support for seventy-two hours before "pulling the plug."

On Monday, the doctors told me that there was still no change and that there probably wouldn't be any. Darrell was still on life support.

On Tuesday morning, Darrell's family was going to decide if they were going to have him cremated. To everyone's surprise, Darrell opened his eyes and started moving them around. The doctors said that even though he had opened his eyes, he was still "brain dead." But he followed every command they gave him. Later that day, miraculously, Darrell started talking. He had a brain all right! He said that he was starving and wanted to be disconnected from life support so that he could eat—he wanted M&Ms,

pancakes, barbecue and ice cream. The doctors said that the odds of Darrell's surviving were something like ninety-nine to one. They just couldn't believe his recovery.

A lot of people were chanting for him. The support of his friends really overwhelmed me. While people were chanting for Darrell, I got a wonderful feeling not to worry, just to keep chanting.

After waking up, I remember how wonderful it felt to be able to lead evening prayers in my hospital room. I chanted with such renewed appreciation. I was alive! I guess since my brain had been deprived of oxygen for nearly twenty minutes, the doctors didn't have much hope for me being more than just a vegetable, if I survived at all. I guess you could say that I got my "red socks" wish that day.

On Sunday, I moved out of the intensive care unit and to the sixth floor of the hospital. On Monday, I went home.

After surviving my ordeal, I learned that I had a blockage in my heart. After the blockage was cleared, an experimental machine called the "Arctic Sun" was used to cool my body to around ninety-two degrees to induce mild hypothermia in hopes of reducing cellular damage, especially to my brain. Prior to using it on me, only one other person had used this machine; but unfortunately, he had died.

I woke up feeling like, while I was gone, I had plugged into my own Buddha nature. In the three days I spent in that state, I became a different person. Now I see people in a more positive light and catch myself more quickly when I discover that I have negative feelings toward someone. My sense of purpose in life has been revitalized. I am no longer here to accumulate stuff. I am here to plant and cultivate the seed of my own enlightenment and that of others, too. I feel that I am here at this time for a reason, and that's why I didn't die. After the news reports came out about my recovery, many people recognized me and wanted to talk to me. How could I tell them the story without talking about Buddhism?

If I had known the value of connecting life-to-life when I first started practicing Buddhism, I would have seen a lot more of this purpose in my life. But I know better than most that it's never too late to start from exactly where you are. As SGI President Ikeda so eloquently puts it, "Forward! Always forward! This is a basic spirit of Buddhism. . . . We live with our gaze fixed upon the future, not hung up on the past. To advance eternally—this is the essence of life and the essence of what it means to be a practitioner of Nichiren Buddhism."

The old Darrell Griffin died in that emergency room. All I want to do now is to promote interest in this wonderful Buddhist philosophy, to encourage people so they might see their own enlightened nature and live their own dreams.

My doctor tells me that only one of the four sides of my heart is functioning, and that it's only working at 10 percent capacity. But I am not the least bit afraid. There is only that much more to prove. I wake up every day feeling that I have more to do. Now in my fifties, there are certainly things I want to accomplish in my lifetime.

I feel more confident within myself. I don't feel that over-coming death was that big of a deal. It was just a wake-up call for me. While I was patient with people before, I'm even more patient now. I don't give advice anymore, I just offer invitations for people to come and chant. My motivation is no longer intellectual. Now when I invite people to practice Nichiren Buddhism, it comes from my heart—my spiritual heart that beats with 100 percent perfection.

CHANTING CAN HELP ANYONE
MAHOGANY GAMBLE

The Buddha knows no path of living apart
from that of living with compassion.
—JOSEI TODA

I GREW UP NOT KNOWING my biological father. In fact, one of the last things I remember about him was him visiting me, taking me to the beach and then promising to give me twenty dollars—a big deal for a five-year-old. I never got the money, nor did I ever see him again. He was a drug dealer and drug user and was often in danger. From time to time, we would hear from his family that he had been shot or imprisoned for his actions.

My mom, after taking my sister and me away from our dad to start a new life, worked hard to raise us. She was introduced to Nichiren Buddhism and began chanting Nam-myoho-renge-kyo shortly after we moved to San Francisco.

My sister and I are ten years apart in age, so it must have been difficult for my mom to raise a toddler and a teenager. While she was working multiple jobs so that we could eat, I spent a lot of time with my father's extended family. There, I was physically, verbally and emotionally abused. My mother never knew how they treated me, and I associated their treatment with my father—I blamed him.

For many years, I was angry and miserable. Not until my mom met my stepdad did I realize that much of my anger and unhappiness stemmed from my experience—or lack of it—with my father. I had intense feelings of hatred toward my stepdad, yet he was one of the kindest, calmest and most generous people I'd met. But my anger toward "dad-types" kept me from appreciating his generosity. Even though I had started chanting by this point, being the spoiled and destructive stepchild I was, I often acted disrespectfully.

Then I got sick. My gallbladder became impacted with gallstones, and I'd be in excruciating pain after every meal. I decided to have my gallbladder removed. After surgery, I had a near-death experience in the hospital. From that point on, I decided to truly *live* life. I wanted to be happy and feel like my life had a purpose. I shared this with a Buddhist friend of mine who visited me, and on a return visit she gave me the book *Discussions on Youth*, a dialogue between SGI President Ikeda and youth leaders in the Soka Gakkai.

Throughout the book, President Ikeda talks a lot about having a mission, and I came to see that my mission was to learn how to become happy and help many others find their happiness. He also emphasizes that youth should have appreciation for their parents. When I first read this, I became angry just thinking about my father. I thought it was impossible that I could ever appreciate him. Yet something about the idea of appreciating him struck a chord with me. I read the portions about appreciating parents again and again.

I talked to a friend, and she asked if I was chanting for my dad. It hadn't even entered my mind. But from that day,

I began chanting for his happiness and for him to change his life and win over the darkness that was causing him to suffer. Once I faced my feelings about my father, it allowed me to open up to my stepdad, and we built a great relationship.

When my biological father died, I felt so many different things: grief, guilt for not being there, anger over the past. Though we hadn't been in contact, I felt connected to him through my chanting for him. When he died, I felt like something in me had died, too. I just needed to know in my heart that he experienced joy in his life and that somehow I was a good daughter to him. I chanted and chanted for my father.

Through chanting, my feelings changed. For the first time I felt true appreciation for my father. Though he had brought suffering to my mom, had he not done so, she never would have moved to San Francisco, where, because of that suffering, she started to practice Nichiren Buddhism. And my father had given me my life, which I now dedicate to helping others become happy.

In the days after my father died, we found out from his sister that he had changed his life. He didn't die an angry drug addict or dealer but a business owner and good-natured person. Hearing this, I felt the power of chanting Nam-myoho-renge-kyo; I could impact my father's life just through chanting. Now, even though he's gone, my efforts in the SGI to help others can further help him find happiness as well.

The Deepest Loss

Aiko Matsumura

Prayer is not a feeble consolation; it is
a powerful, unyielding conviction.
—Daisaku Ikeda

I WAS BORN THE SECOND DAUGHTER of a well-off family and lived my life without ever having to struggle much for anything. I was bright and happy, with a tenacious, never-give-up attitude. I loved literature, and when I was in high school, I had an essay published in a local newspaper. "Life is long," I wrote, "and in the future there may come a time when the harsh winds of fate bear down upon me as strong as a typhoon, but one should never grieve or be defeated. Life is determined by how bravely we face it and how we create it."

A boy named Takaetsu read my essay and was touched by it. We became pen pals and eventually married. Later, he decided to adopt my faith in Nichiren Buddhism.

I was twenty when we married and my life changed completely, because my husband's family were farmers. Besides being a farmer's wife, I worked in sales and was president of the local Parent Teacher Association. I also volunteered a lot of my time in SGI Buddhist activities and took on demanding responsibilities. The driving power in my busy life was the Buddhist practice of chanting Nam-myoho-renge-kyo, which my husband and I participated in together, daily.

Then something occurred which I could have never have imagined. My son had broken up with his girlfriend and had become very depressed. He felt deceived by her. He stopped going to work and shut himself away in his room. Because he wasn't going to work, he was fired from his job and his depression worsened. I hoped he would snap out of it, and I told him he needed to be stronger; there were lots of girls he could go out with.

On October 16, I received a call from the police. When my husband and I arrived at the hospital, my son's body was laid out on a bed with a sheet covering his face. He had jumped from the building in which his girlfriend lived. He was twenty-seven.

At first I was angry. How could he have done this? Was he that weak? Then immediately I realized I should not blame him. Day and night I cried. I did not realize how much he had been suffering. I could have been more compassionate, I told myself; I could have shared his pain. Now it was too late to do anything.

Time stopped for me. For months I could not bear to face anyone.

No matter how old a parent grows, their child is always their child and a parent should never outlive their children. Everything about our short history together recurred to me vividly. Most painful was a message he wrote to me on Mother's Day when he was in the fifth grade. "Dear Mom, I will grow up. You are always scolding me. Please also praise me sometimes, too. I am so happy when you smile at me. I promise you that I will give you a comfortable life when I grow up. You are always working so hard. Please take good care of yourself, Mom. Love always." I wanted to tell him now, "I am so sorry for always being so strict with you. I was always scolding you." Why was I not more kind to my son? Day after day I tortured myself with these regrets.

Just as I had not been able to understand my son's struggle, I now felt as though there was no one in the world who could understand the pain I was feeling.

One day, I started having difficulty breathing; I broke into a cold sweat and fainted. When I came to, I was in the hospital, and my husband was standing over me with an anxious look on his face. He told me, "You can't go on like this. There are people who need you. You have to take care of yourself." The love in his face and the gentleness of his words touched me and shone some light into the darkness of my heart.

I continued to chant for a way out of my pain. As my chanting deepened, my perception of my son's death slowly began to change. Gradually, I began to feel as though the frozen river of my life was thawing and starting to move again.

The knowledge from my Buddhist practice that death is not merely the absence of life but, together with life, is an essential part of a deeper continuum started to take root in my heart. It eased the pain and helped the thaw.

I started to feel that I wanted to celebrate my son's twenty-seven years of life and to help him leave behind his legacy. My nightly tears were not the legacy I wanted for him.

I had always enjoyed writing. After chanting about this, I began to write. I chanted, wrote, scratched out what I had written, tried again and then chanted some more. Though I had thought I had some talent for literature, I realized now how difficult writing can be. It took one year, but I finally finished the biography of my son and me.

I dedicated the book to my son and my mother, who left me these words before she died: "Cherry blossoms only come into bloom after enduring the long, cold winter. The warmth of spring can only be appreciated by enduring the frozen air of winter. Live your life like the cherry blossom, which comes into full, vivid flower in the beauty of spring."

The book was published. To my surprise, I received so many responses; some from mothers who had had similar experiences to mine. I was not alone.

Our exchange of letters led eventually to the formation of a network of mothers called the Cherry Blossom Group. Through this group I have been able to give back to others the kind of support that I myself experienced from my Buddhist women friends. They came to my aid in my darkest hours, not only by offering me words of support and prayers but by sitting with me and sharing my grief. Not everyone has this kind of invaluable support and yet I, and my son, had been able to create this group where suffering mothers could find love, support and eventually peace. This was my son's legacy.

The death of my son taught me the power of faith. I don't have to say goodbye to him; rather I say, "Thank you." I feel I am just now beginning to blossom. And I know that the light of spring, the light of hope and the precious memory of him will always be in my heart.

Changing Course

Maureen Cervelli

Live your beliefs and you can turn the world around.
—Henry David Thoreau

M Y PARENTS WERE HIGH SCHOOL sweethearts and deeply in love. They survived World War II and were determined to build the beautiful American family. Proud Irish Catholics, they moved to a newly established suburb just south of San Francisco in 1951, a few months before I was born. My parents had six daughters, all less than two years apart; I was the third born.

Soon, the American dream faded. In the 1950s, it was fashionable to have cocktails every evening and my mother began to drink. By the time I was five years old, my mother was a full-blown alcoholic—always red in the face and unsteady. Family, church and community were in a typical 1950s state of denial. My youngest sister died shortly after birth from alcoholic complications. After her death, my mother was inconsolable.

My father worked two jobs to keep up with the bills. My mother didn't function. My older sisters would go to school, sometimes coming home to find the youngest still in the diapers from the night before. My dad, angry and frustrated, repeated a pattern he learned from his own father—violence. This became an everyday experience. My older sisters and I would crouch behind the couch and peek out as we watched the beatings. I remember, after one such incident, my dad threw my mother out of the house with no clothes on and locked the door. Shame, guilt and self-hatred became the elements of our young lives.

My mother would often gather us girls around a small coffee table to pray the rosary. She'd say, "Let's pray that Mommy won't be sick."

Unfortunately, my mother always got sick, and when I was eight, my mother died at home in her sleep as a result of a head injury. She was only thirty-six.

My father continued to raise us to the best of his ability. From frustration and lacking any other strategy however, he would often communicate with his belt. My dad married a young woman from Ireland. At twelve years old, I thought my dreams had come true. Now I would have a wonderful mother who would tell me stories and teach me how to curl my hair.

Instead, our stepmother could not accept her new role. My parents ate separate meals from us and we basically continued to live a less than happy family life. Needless to say, by the time each one of us turned eighteen, we moved out of the house. One bright spot happened in my life, however, when I was fifteen. I met Steven, a nice Italian Catholic boy. Like my parents, we became high school sweethearts.

First to leave home was my oldest sister, Kathy. She moved to San Francisco where she was introduced to Nichiren Buddhism. Kathy passionately told me about her new faith. She desperately wanted me to chant. Even though I was "a very good Catholic," I started secretly chanting when I was sixteen. In San Francisco, the summer of my high school graduation, Steven and I each became Buddhists and members of the SGI-USA.

A few months after that, I became pregnant. I was barely eighteen years old and in total hell. What would I do? Abortion was not legal; anyway, I was still way "too Catholic" for that.

More than fear of my church, or my father, was my fear of being a mother. I didn't know what a mother was. I didn't know what a happy family was. I was encouraged to chant for a happy family—for my deepest dream to come true. But what began as my biggest nightmare became my first and most exceptional blessing. Steven and I married and I gave birth to our beautiful daughter, Erin.

In early May, Kathy called me to share her daily encouragement. She spoke at length one lunch hour about one Buddhist concept. In particular, she wanted me to understand one of the worst stumbling blocks of any faith: the death of a young believer. Over and over again, she told me to never be swayed by this kind of circumstance. I distinctly remember smiling when I promised her "I will never be swayed, I love you—goodbye."

Days later, on the way home from a Buddhist meeting, Kathy, twenty-three, was killed in a car accident. The news of her death was shocking and unbelievable. I immediately began to chant to the Gohonzon as tears rolled down my cheeks. That night, Steven and I vowed never to stop our Buddhist practice *no matter what*. I don't know where our pledge came from—until that moment, I didn't think

I had faith. Nine months later, in February, our loving son, Emmett, was born.

After my sister's death, something profound happened in my family among my dad, my stepmother and my sisters. We started developing an amazingly close relationship of love, trust and genuine appreciation. I realized then just how much my sister Kathy had served our family.

For the next five years, Steven and I worked hard to help the SGI-USA grow in San Jose. We continued with our promise not to give up. I held on to my dream for a happy family.

Then at twenty-four, I experienced the reality of my married life. I fell out of love with my husband. I was tormented, and I hated my life. Steven is a kind and gentle man, but I was certain that I didn't love him anymore. I didn't want to be married. I didn't want to be a mother. I didn't know what I wanted, except to escape and be happy.

I remembered how much my parents were in love once, and how their love got buried in the day-to-day struggle of living. I realized how deep and painful my family propensity was.

One day, after reading SGI President Ikeda's encouragement to study the writings of Nichiren Daishonin, I opened the letter "Many in Body, One in Mind." One sentence jumped out of the page and into my life: "Even an individual at cross purposes with himself is certain to end in failure." That was me! I was at "cross purposes." I had to take responsibility for that. I prayed to embrace and make a final decision—and I did. I decided to stay in my marriage.

Once I did that, things moved rather quickly. About six months later, our marriage was on the mend. But *I* hadn't healed; my fundamental, profound changes had barely just begun. I realized I was an angry, unhappy, insecure young woman. I behaved like a brat most of the time. I worked to reestablish an intimate relationship with my husband and to appreciate even the smallest things he did. I challenged myself to become the "queen" of appreciation. This process of deepening my appreciation became even more challenging when my children became adolescents.

Two years later, I went to Japan with an SGI-USA group where I met Daisaku Ikeda. He looked deep into my eyes and wrote these words down, "With family harmony, this life will be protected." He struck a chord deep in my heart. Until then, I had been afraid I would—like my mother and my sister—also die young. Until then, I had been afraid I would not have a happy family. President Ikeda saw in me what I could not. At twenty-nine, I wanted to live the happiest life as a wife, mother, daughter, sister and Buddhist. I will always be grateful for those sincere words that he wrote for me.

Steven and I have created a life filled with love and family fortune. We feel deep appreciation to SGI President Ikeda for encouraging us to grow, to study and to experience the beauty and struggle of life in this one-of-a-kind organization called the SGI. Without it I was destined to follow my family's pattern—I had no other options. Buddhism allowed me to change the course of my life and the lives of my future generations.

I will never forget that I stand on the shoulders of those who came before me, especially my sister Kathy. She lived her life according to Buddhist writings. She sought joy in every circumstance in order to strengthen the power of her faith and was then able to give that joy to those around her. Her legacy will live on forever.

9/11

GEORGE AOYAMA

If we are to survive, a stronghold of peace must be
fashioned within the mind of every single man, woman
and child on the earth. This stronghold must resolutely
hold out against the invasion of an idea to make war.

—DAISAKU IKEDA

W HEN I WAS SEVENTEEN YEARS OLD, I heard
that my father was on board a plane that a group
of terrorists hijacked. It was September 11, 2001. The first
thing I did was to chant for his safety. At this time, my
father's death was not yet confirmed. I chanted with all of
my heart to send my prayers and energy to him, hoping
from the depth of my life that he would be OK. I also
prayed that I would have the courage to be brave, no matter what the outcome.

After I realized the inevitable and eventually accepted
my father's death, I thought that now, more than ever, I
would need to succeed in my own life. I thought that if I
lose to the suffering caused by his death and live a life of
victimization, I would have wasted all the effort my father
put into raising me to be a great individual.

As I faced his death, people who immediately came to
support our family were the members of the SGI-USA, and
my father's Buddhist friends and co-workers. They offered
as much help as they could provide. They shared with us

how much they loved my father and how much they too were agonizing over his death. They told us how sincerely he had worked and told us stories of his profound and amazing life. Their experiences and feelings allowed me to understand what kind of person my father was.

I was very grateful to hear their soothing words. I was inspired by the way my father had lived and who he was. As many SGI-USA members told me, he was very bright and caring. His co-workers told me that he was very insightful, precise and diligent at work.

I, myself, remembered how compassionate he was with our family. As a teenager, I would spend more time with him than I did with my friends because he wanted our time together to be special. I realized that not only was I fostered by his caring words of wisdom, but I was also nurtured by simply being with him. He often said about my sister and me, "If George and Emily are happy, I am happy too." He took great care of his family and his love for me remains, even after his death.

My father worked for the SGI-USA and propagated humanism. His work responsibilities would require that he drive many hours and fly in and out of the country to encourage people, and he loved it. He was working for world peace through individual peace and personal happiness. This is why he was on the plane on September 11.

One of the passengers on the same plane with my father had called home that day just before the plane crashed into the North Tower. The family member who received the call said that they could hear someone on board chanting. My father had been working until the last moment of his life for the sake of peace and no doubt trying to calm the other passengers. Because of the way my father loved his family, and the people he worked with and for, and because he lived such a happy and fulfilling life, I am encouraged every day to live strongly and to follow his example.

SGI President Ikeda had also quickly responded with prayers and messages of compassion. I was touched by how much care he provides to a single individual. His love, as well as the members' support, gave me a deep awareness of how profound Buddhism is.

Nichiren Buddhism teaches that although people die, life is eternal. This understanding of life and death has helped me. Knowing that death is not an end but a departure to a new life has given me a peace of mind I would not otherwise have. Moreover, through Buddhism, I have been able to have such a wonderful connection with my father because our relationship carries with it the basis of a shared faith.

The practice of Nichiren Buddhism entails an eternal mission for world peace and to dispel all kinds of misery from this earth. For this reason, the connection my father and I have can never be destroyed. I, like my father, am dedicated to the cause of human happiness, because that's the way to eventually bring family peace, community peace and eventually world peace.

I asked myself, "What must I, and will I do, as a victim of terrorism?" I did not want anybody to experience what I had to go through: to lose a loved one, a person who was innocent. I did not want to let such a tragedy happen again. There are many people around the world who are suffering as a result of various forms of violence. My deep desire is to eliminate human misery as much as I can. I am determined to wage peace and stand up for non-violence.

Determined to carry on my father's spirit and contribute to society through the propagation of humanism, I enrolled at Soka University of America, Aliso Viejo, in August of 2003. Founded by SGI President Ikeda, it is a university that is dedicated to fostering truly capable leaders. I chose the philosophy of Soka education to become a global citizen to promote the spread of peace, culture, education and the sanctity of life. My father had studied at Soka High School and Soka University in Japan.

Throughout my first academic year at SUA, the more I challenged myself to develop my intellectual abilities and cultivate my character, the stronger and closer I felt to my father's spirit.

I faced many challenges in academics and human relationships. My first step was to chant earnestly to bring out my wisdom. When I could not accomplish as much as I wanted to in academics, or when the assignments were overwhelming, I reminded myself what President Ikeda taught us students, "The purpose of academics is to cultivate one's self—it is for the people. No matter how slow the progress may be, it is important to advance even if it's a single step and have the spirit to keep challenging yourself." I am determined to work for human happiness, as was the purpose of my father's life, rather than perpetrate more hate and fear by harboring anger and a desire for revenge against the people who took his life. It is a constant choice but one that is easier to make when I follow the example of my father's life.

I want my father's legacy to live through me. Consequently, I study and explore ideas and philosophy, forge dialogue and seek peace through meaningful interaction with people. That's how my father did it, and that's what he *loved* and what brought him joy.

My challenges at SUA have helped me develop these qualities I aspire to—qualities that friends and comrades have attributed to my father. He was a very warm-hearted and insightful person who brightened his environment and inspired people. He seriously and diligently worked and dedicated his efforts to support people's happiness. I try to do the same and follow his example, and it has enhanced my own life. My dedication is possible because my father is, and always will be, in my heart.

putting it all into practice

Reprinted from *The Buddha in Your Mirror*

OVER THE COURSE OF THIS BOOK, we've discussed how the key to surmounting life's hurdles and achieving its goals lies within each of us, the Buddhas in our respective mirrors. We've examined the interconnection between ourselves and others, and between our lives and our respective environments. We've even explored how to face death in a fresh, encouraging way. The crucial step now is putting into practice what we've learned, making the thrilling leap from the mere holding of knowledge to the actualization of our vast potential. As we've said, Buddhism is reason, and what's more reasonable than being asked to put stock in something only after we have received proof of its effectiveness?

The primary practice, as we have explained throughout the book, is to chant Nam-myoho-renge-kyo.

The Mechanics of Chanting

Nam-myoho-renge-kyo can be chanted anywhere at any time—preferably in a manner that won't disturb others—but the effects of practice are best seen when carried out on a regular basis. We suggest setting aside a bit of time each morning and evening for, say, at least five minutes each session. Sit straight and comfortably, and, if possible, face a blank portion of the wall or some neutral background that won't distract you. Place your palms together at chest level, fingers pointing upward with the tips at just about the level of your chin.

>   As to pronunciation:
>   Nam–the a has the sound of the a in *father*
>   Myo–think of it as placing an m before one
>   half of *yo-yo*
>   Ho–like the garden implement *hoe*
>   Ren–like the bird *wren*
>   Ge–sounds like the word *get* without the t
>   Kyo–similar to *myo*
>   Each syllable gets one equal stress or beat:
>   Nám myó hó rén gé kyó

The chant repeats without a break between each Nam-myoho-renge-kyo. Feel free, of course, to breathe whenever necessary, then go back to your rhythmic chant. Try to maintain an even tone and rhythm, but don't be overly concerned about it as you will settle into it naturally in a short time. You can either focus on a specific goal or problem, or you can let your mind naturally coast from thought to thought. You will soon see some tangible result.

Again, this is not to say that you must have conviction that this will happen from the very start. It is only natural to have doubt. Confidence in Buddhist practice begins with your very first attempt to "try it and see." And it deepens over time as you gain continual, actual proof. Yet doubt is an element with which practitioners must always contend. As the German author Hermann Hesse said: "Faith and doubt correspond to each other and supplement each other. There is no true faith where there is no doubt."

The essential thing, however, is to use your doubts as fuel to find the answers to your questions. Practically speaking, it helps if you can bolster your practice by relating to like-minded others who can encourage you through life's inevitable rough spots, and whom you can encourage in turn based on your own emerging experiences. As this book has pointed out, we don't live in a vacuum, and our efforts to help others become happy directly enhance our own level of happiness.

If you'd like to take things a step (or thirty-seven) further, there is a vast community of Nichiren Buddhists to assist you in your great experiment. The SGI-USA holds discussion meetings and cultural activities in all fifty states as well as throughout the Caribbean, on Guam and other Pacific islands. Most meetings are informal and held in practitioners' homes. Through the community of fellow Buddhists, you can take the next step of learning about the supplementary practice, the twice-daily recitation of portions of two chapters of the Lotus Sutra, which bolsters one's daily chanting of Nam-myoho-renge-kyo. This aspect of practice requires some tricky pronunciations, and an experienced guide can be invaluable. You can also receive the Gohonzon, or "object of devotion" to focus on while you chant. The Gohonzon enables you to fuse your subjective wisdom with the objective reality of the universe.

Having a Buddhist friend to guide you along the way is exceedingly helpful in maintaining your practice, and the SGI-USA provides a structure for making just such a friend (or many). In fact, through the umbrella organization SGI, you can find friends and activities (some twelve million practitioners in more than 190 countries and territories) throughout the world. For information about meetings and activities in your area, you can call the SGI-USA headquarters in Santa Monica, California, at 1-310-260-8900. Or visit its Web site: www.sgi-usa.org

At the beginning of this book, we spoke of each individual's limitless potential for wisdom, courage, hope, confidence, compassion, vitality and endurance. The adventure begins the very first time you chant Nam-myoho-renge-kyo and introduce yourself to the Buddha in your mirror.

glossary

Buddha: "Awakened One." One who perceives the true nature of all life and leads others to attain this same enlightenment. This Buddha nature exists in all beings and is characterized by the qualities of wisdom, courage, compassion and life force.

Buddhahood: The state that a Buddha has attained. The ultimate goal of Buddhist practice. The word *enlightenment* is often used synonymously with Buddhahood. Buddhahood is regarded as a state of perfect freedom, in which one is awakened to the eternal and ultimate truth that is the reality of all things. This supreme state of life is characterized by boundless wisdom and infinite compassion. The Lotus Sutra reveals that Buddhahood is a potential in the lives of all beings.

Buddha nature: The inherent Buddhahood that exists in all life.

Bodhisattva: One who aspires to enlightenment, or Buddhahood. *Bodhi* means enlightenment, and *sattva*, a living being. A person who aspires to enlightenment and carries out altruistic practice. The predominant characteristic of a bodhisattva is therefore compassion.

Buddhist altar: The primary purpose of the altar in Nichiren Buddhism is to protect the Gohonzon. SGI members often adorn their altars with candles, incense, evergreens and more as a gesture of appreciation for benefits received through Buddhist practice. Other accessories such as beads are also used when chanting.

devils: In Buddhism, devils represent the destructive and debilitating forces within a person's life that hinder a person's Buddhist practice.

301

They are not actual sentient beings but metaphors for delusional life-states.

earthly desires are enlightenment: *Earthly desires* is a generic term for all the workings of life, including desires and illusions in the general sense, that cause one's psychological and physical suffering and impede the quest for enlightenment. In many forms of Buddhism, earthy desires are meant to be extinguished, but in Nichiren Buddhism they are viewed as the impetus for changing one's life-state.

Gohonzon: The object of devotion in Nichiren Buddhism. In the form of a written scroll, it is the embodiment of the Law of Nam-myoho-renge-kyo, expressing the life-state of Buddhahood, which all people inherently possess. *Go* means "worthy of honor" and *honzon* means "object of fundamental respect."

human revolution: A concept indicating the self-reformation of an individual—the strengthening of life force and the establishment of Buddhahood—that is the goal of Buddhist practice.

Daisaku Ikeda: President of the Soka Gakkai International. Prolific writer, poet and peace activist, he is recognized as one of the leading interpreters of Buddhism and spiritual leader for millions worldwide.

Lotus Sutra: The highest teaching of Shakyamuni Buddha, it reveals that all people can attain enlightenment and declares that his former teachings should be regarded as preparatory.

karma: Potentials in the inner, unconscious realm of life created through one's actions in the past or present that manifest themselves as various results in the present or future. Karma is a variation of the Sanskrit *karman,* which means act, action, a former act leading to a future result, or result. One's thought, speech and behavior, both good and bad, imprint themselves as a latent force or potential in one's life. This latent force, or karma, when activated by an external stimulus, produces a corresponding good or bad effect, i.e., happiness or suffering. There are also neutral acts that produce neither good nor bad results. According to this concept of karma, one's actions in the past have shaped one's present reality, and one's actions in the present will in turn influence one's future. The Buddhist doctrine of karma is not fatalistic. Rather, karma is viewed not only as a means to explain the present but also as the potential force through which to influence one's future. No ill karma is so fixed or predetermined that Buddhist practice in the present cannot transform it for the better.

kosen-rufu: Literally, to widely declare and spread (Buddhism); to secure lasting peace and happiness for all humankind through the propagation of Nichiren Buddhism. More broadly, *kosen-rufu* refers to the process of establishing the humanistic ideals of Nichiren Buddhism in society.

life-condition: The overall state of one's life, which affects how one views and influences current circumstances. Through practicing Nichiren Buddhism, people can strengthen their life-condition, thus finding greater hope and optimism while also generating the power to affect positive change in their environment.

Tsunesaburo Makiguchi: Author, educator and first president of the Soka Gakkai. His theory of value-creating education, which he published in book form in 1930, is centered on a belief in the unlimited potential of every individual and regards education as the lifelong pursuit of self-awareness, wisdom and development. Makiguchi died in prison during World War II for opposing the Japanese government's totalitarian social policies, specifically the enforcement of Shinto as the state religion.

Mystic Law: The ultimate principle of Nichiren's teachings. Mystic Law is the English translation of *myoho*, as in Nam-myoho-renge-kyo. *Myo* means mystic or wonderful, and *ho* means Buddhist Law, or dharma.

Nam-myoho-renge-kyo: The ultimate Law of the true aspect of life permeating all phenomena in the universe. The invocation established by Nichiren Daishonin on April 28, 1253. Nichiren teaches that this phrase encompasses all laws and teachings within itself, and that the benefit of chanting Nam-myoho-renge-kyo includes the benefit of conducting all virtuous practices. *Nam* means "devotion to"; *myoho* means "Mystic Law"; *renge* refers to the lotus flower, which simultaneously blooms and seeds, indicating the simultaneity of cause and effect; *kyo* means "sutra," the teaching of a Buddha.

Nichiren Daishonin: The thirteenth-century Japanese Buddhist teacher and reformer who taught that all people have the potential for enlightenment. He defined the universal Law as Nam-myoho-renge-kyo and established the Gohonzon as the object of devotion for all people to attain Buddhahood.

poison into medicine: The transformation of destructive tendencies and circumstances into positive events and good fortune through practicing Nichiren Buddhism. Rather than focus on ways to evade problems, Nichiren taught that problems can be faced directly, overcome and changed into a source of happiness.

Soka Gakkai International: A worldwide Buddhist association that promotes peace and individual happiness based on the teachings of Nichiren Daishonin, with more than twelve million members in one hundred ninety countries and territories. Its headquarters is in Tokyo, Japan.

Shakyamuni: Also, Siddhartha Gautama. Born in southern Nepal about twenty-five hundred years ago, he is the first recorded Buddha and founder of Buddhism. For fifty years, he expounded various sutras (teachings), culminating in the Lotus Sutra.

Josei Toda: The second president of the Soka Gakkai. After the devastation of World War II, he transformed the Soka Gakkai from a small group of educators to a major religious organization. At the time of his death, the Soka Gakkai surpassed 750,000 families. His disciple and successor, Daisaku Ikeda, continued Toda's mission and led the Soka Gakkai International to become one of the largest and most diverse lay Buddhist organizations in the world today.

more on
nichiren buddhism
and its application
to daily life

THE FOLLOWING EIGHT TITLES can be purchased from your local or on-line bookseller, or go to the Middleway Press Web site (www.middlewaypress.com).

BUDDHISM DAY BY DAY: WISDOM FOR MODERN LIFE
by Daisaku Ikeda
This treasury of practical information and encouragement will appeal to those seeking a deeper understanding of how to apply the tenets of Nichiren Buddhism in their day-to-day lives.
(Paperback: ISBN 978-0-9723267-5-9; $15.95)

BUDDHISM FOR YOU SERIES
In this oasis of insight and advice on the power of Nichiren Buddhism—which holds that everyone has a Buddha nature of limitless power, wisdom, and compassion—readers will learn how to live a life filled with courage, determination, love and prayer to achieve their goals and desires. Author Daisaku Ikeda, one of the world's foremost Buddhist philosophers, demystifies the essence of Buddhist scriptures, in short, easy-to-read entries, making them applicable to the challenge of daily life.
(COURAGE Hardcover: ISBN 978-0-9723267-6-6; $7.95)

(DETERMINATION Hardcover: ISBN 978-0-9723267-8-0; $7.95)
(LOVE Hardcover: ISBN 978-0-9723267-7-3; $7.95)
(PRAYER Hardcover: ISBN 978-0-9723267-9-7; $7.95)

THE BUDDHA IN YOUR MIRROR:
PRACTICAL BUDDHISM AND THE SEARCH FOR SELF,
by Woody Hochswender, Greg Martin and Ted Morino

A bestselling Buddhist primer that reveals the most modern, effective and practical way to achieve what is called enlightenment or Buddhahood. Based on the centuries-old teaching of the Japanese Buddhist master Nichiren, this method has been called the "direct path" to enlightenment.
(Paperback: ISBN 0-978-9674697-8-2; $14.00,
Hardcover: ISBN 0-978-9674697-1-3; $23.95)

CHOOSE HOPE: YOUR ROLE IN
WAGING PEACE IN THE NUCLEAR AGE
by David Krieger and Daisaku Ikeda

"In this nuclear age, when the future of humankind is imperiled by irrational strategies, it is imperative to restore sanity to our policies and hope to our destiny. Only a rational analysis of our problems can lead to their solution. This book is an example par excellence of a rational approach."
—JOSEPH ROTBLAT, Nobel Peace Prize laureate
(Hardcover: ISBN 978-0-9674697-6-8; $23.95)

PLANETARY CITIZENSHIP: YOUR VALUES, BELIEFS
AND ACTIONS CAN SHAPE A SUSTAINABLE WORLD
by Hazel Henderson and Daisaku Ikeda

"*Planetary Citizenship* is a delightful introduction to some of the most important ideas and facts concerning stewardship of the planet. I cannot think of any book that deals with more important issues."
—MIHALY CSIKSZENTMIHALYI, author of *Flow: The Psychology of Optimal Experience*, California
(Hardcover: ISBN 978-0-9723267-2-8; $23.95)

Romancing the Buddha:
Embracing Buddhism in My Everyday Life
by Michael Lisagor

"*Romancing the Buddha: Embracing Buddhism in My Everyday Life* is
. . . a resource which provides excellent insights into applying Nichiren
Buddhism to the difficulties of daily life, including depression, spousal
illness, the challenge of raising two daughters and the quest for happiness. An absorbing and inspirational selection of vignettes touched with
wisdom, *Romancing the Buddha* is an impressive and welcome contribution to Buddhist Studies reading lists."
—Midwest Book Review
(Paperback: ISBN 978-0-9723267-4-2; $18.95)

Unlocking the Mysteries of Birth & Death . . .
and Everything in Between, A Buddhist View
of Life (second edition)
by Daisaku Ikeda

"In this slender volume, Ikeda presents a wealth of profound information in a clear and straightforward style that can be easily absorbed by
the interested lay reader. His life's work, and the underlying purpose of
his book, is simply to help human beings derive maximum meaning
from their lives through the study of Buddhism."
—ForeWord Magazine
(Paperback: ISBN 978-0-9723267-0-4; $15.00)

The Way of Youth: Buddhist Common Sense
for Handling Life's Questions,
by Daisaku Ikeda

"[This book] shows the reader how to flourish as a young person in the
world today; how to build confidence and character in modern society;
learn to live with respect for oneself and others; how to contribute to a
positive, free and peaceful society; and find true personal happiness."
—Midwest Book Review
(Paperback: ISBN 978-0-9674697-0-6; $14.95)

green
press
INITIATIVE

Printed on recycled paper.

MIDDLEWAY PRESS is committed to preserving ancient forest and natural resources. We are a member of the Green Press Initiative—a nonprofit program dedicated to supporting book publishers in maximizing their use of fiber, which is not sourced from ancient or endangered forests. We have elected to print this title on Glatfelter Thor PCW, made with 30 percent post consumer waste, processed chlorine free. By using this paper, we are saving the following:

42 fully grown trees
15,258 gallons of water
29 million BTUs of energy
1,959 pounds of solid waste
3,676 pounds of greenhouse gases

For more information about the Green Press Initiative and the use of recycled paper in book publishing, visit www.greenpressinitiative.org